Managing Corpo
Diverse National Cultures

MW01027106

How should a Western company manage cross-culturally corporate values in its foreign subsidiaries? Do these values make sense everywhere and can they be assumed to be universal or, on the contrary, are they culturally Western specific?

Philippe d'Iribarne provides answers to these timely and urgent questions, based on research carried out in the subsidiaries of a leading global company, Lafarge, in the contrasting cultural environments of China, the United States, France, and Jordan. It appears that, in a large part of the world, people's expectations are similar; they expect from a good employer clear and decisive leadership, and fair and compassionate treatment, helping them to live a good life. But treating these expectations as the "same" could be misleading. Western companies with a humanistic orientation are well positioned to fulfil them, provided they are willing, in each and every geography, to take into account the local vision of the right way to achieve a good life.

By following the example presented in this book, companies who care can deliver economic efficiency as well as progressive people management in the countries in which they operate.

Philippe d'Iribarne is Managing Director of Gestion et Société (Management and Society), at CNRS (National Center for Scientific Research) in Paris, France.

Routledge Studies in Management, Organizations, and Society

This series presents innovative work grounded in new realities, addressing issues crucial to an understanding of the contemporary world. This is the world of organized societies, where boundaries between formal and informal, public and private, local and global organizations have been displaced or have vanished, along with other nineteenth-century dichotomies and oppositions. Management, apart from becoming a specialized profession for a growing number of people, is an everyday activity for most members of modern societies.

Similarly, at the level of enquiry, culture and technology, and literature and economics, can no longer be conceived as isolated intellectual fields; conventional canons and established mainstreams are contested. *Management, Organization, and Society* addresses these contemporary dynamics of transformation in a manner that transcends disciplinary boundaries, with books that will appeal to researchers, students, and practitioners alike.

Managing Corporate Values in Diverse National Cultures

The challenge of differences

Philippe d'Iribarne

Routledge
Taylor & Francis Group

LONDON AND NEW YORK

English language edition first published 2012
by Routledge
2 Park Square, Milton Park, Abingdon, Oxon OX14 4RN

Simultaneously published in the USA and Canada
by Routledge
711 Third Avenue, New York, NY 10017

First issued in paperback 2017

Routledge is an imprint of the Taylor & Francis Group, an informa business

© 2012 Editions du Seuil

The right of Philippe d'Iribarne to be identified
as author of this work has been asserted by him
in accordance with sections 77 and 78 of the
Copyright, Designs and Patents Act 1988.

All rights reserved. No part of this book may be reprinted or
reproduced or utilized in any form or by any electronic, mechanical,
or other means, now known or hereafter invented, including photocopying
and recording, or in any information storage or retrieval system,
without permission in writing from the publishers.

Trademark notice: Product or corporate names may be trademarks
or registered trademarks, and are used only for identification and
explanation without intent to infringe.

Originally published under the title *L'Epreuve des différences:
L'expérience d'une entreprise mondiale* © Editions du Seuil, 2009

British Library Cataloguing in Publication Data
A catalogue record for this book is available from the British Library

Library of Congress Cataloging in Publication Data
Iribarne, Philippe d'.
  [Épreuve des différences. English]
  Managing corporate values in diverse national cultures: the
  challenge of differences/Philippe d'Iribarne.
  p. cm.—(Routledge studies in management, organizations, and
  society; 19)
  Originally published as: L'épreuve des différences: l'expérience
  d'une entreprise mondiale. Paris: Seuil, ©2009.
  Includes bibliographical references and index. 1. International
  business enterprises. 2. Globalization. 3. Corporate culture.
  I. Title.
  HD2755.5.I588513 2012
  658'.049—dc23   2011049345

ISBN 13: 978-1-138-11828-7 (pbk)
ISBN 13: 978-0-415-50463-8 (hbk)

Typeset in Times New Roman
by Florence Production Ltd, Stoodleigh, Devon

Contents

viii   *Contents*

Foreword

Lafarge, an industrial group with French roots and a humanist tradition, can celebrate today half a century of international growth: Canada, Brazil, and Morocco in the 1950s, the United States in the 1980s, Europe in the 1990s, and a great many emerging countries from the mid-1990s onwards.

Now operating in nearly eighty countries, the Group has had no difficulty in uniting its teams from highly diverse backgrounds around a technical culture. However, the real challenge to internationalization lies in the multiplicity of national and local cultures that underpin management cultures. Understanding and harnessing this diversity has been a necessary step in creating a common management culture, a common performance culture.

Lafarge has used a step-wise approach, without losing its basic identity, favoring the continuity of change rather than rupture, and enabling as many people as possible to gradually join forces around core values that help create and give meaning to a common and shared identity.

This was the genesis of the Lafarge Group's well-known *Principles of Action* in 1975. These have since been regularly updated to integrate the Group's development and the progress made towards finding this common culture. Backed by successive management teams, they impact behaviors and shape the Group's culture.

The values are robust, the way in which they are expressed and lived dovetailing with the constraints and concerns of the moment; and on the basis of a small number of values, such as courage, commitment, responsibility, surpassing oneself, a sense of interest, and respect for others, it is possible to build a culture of excellence.

The latest update to our *Principles of Action* goes back to 2003. Bertrand Collomb entrusted me with this responsibility before he handed the management team over to me in 2006.

The stakes were clear: how could we draw on our values to find the strengths to develop, beyond a leadership culture, a real performance culture in a group that is not only global but also highly multi-local?

Once this version had been authored and distributed, I decided, just before taking on leadership of the Group, to give top priority to workplace health and safety:

- grounded in our values of respect and humanism;
- based on our course towards excellence; and
- able to mobilize each of the Group's employees.

This was certainly the most important decision I have ever made: it made sense to everyone, it mobilized people. It was this decision that enabled us to make a success of the other priorities and substantially improve our performance.

At various points in time, but above all during our Leader for Tomorrow program, Philippe d'Iribarne found that our chosen pathway offered a field for scientific observation and reflection, and this became the starting point for this book.

The book shows us the complexity between the culture of collaborative work advocated by international corporations and local cultures. It also shows that a firm insistence on certain values or approaches, even though reactions and behavior are not uniform, is likely to secure support, and thus greater efficiency of action.

"Our values have value," as I usually say.

There is little doubt that this book gives us keys to understanding how we can be more efficient. Others will certainly discover here an enriching contribution to the pool of knowledge in an area that is critical for the future: the capacity of diverse local cultures to find pathways leading to cooperation rather than confrontation.

Bruno Lafont
President and CEO
Lafarge

Acknowledgments

I would like to thank all those who made this book possible.

The Lafarge Group, headed by Bertrand Collomb and then Bruno Lafont, which had expressed the desire to have its corporate policy of respect for cultural diversity underpinned by evidence-based knowledge about the encounter between universal values and individual cultures.

Christian Herrault, Operations Executive Vice-President, who was directly responsible for the design and implementation of the research program that emerged as a result of the Group's desire, and who steadfastly accompanied the program through to completion.

All those in the Chinese, Jordanian, and Malay subsidiaries who shared with me their experiences and hopes. Their contributions convey the rich diversity of humanity that this research is seeking to express.

Geneviève Felten, Hèla Yousfi, Jean-Pierre Segal and Mingming Duan, who each gave me valuable support for the various stages of the investigations carried out during the project. Gill Gladstone, whose skillful translation of the original French text integrates the cultural dimension that a change of languages implies.

Introduction

The encounter between different cultures is full of promise and opportunity, but it is only through many challenging experiences that these can come to fruition. What is in question is the capacity of Western modernity, in all its multiple forms, to serve as a beacon for humanity. From China to the Arab world, the existence of a plurality of cultures enjoying equal dignity is now brought to the fore, which thus boomerangs back to the West one of its fundamental values. This reaction, however, is suspected of masking a refusal of values that are well and truly universal, with there being little reason for these to remain confined to the Western world. Does this mean that we are fated to choose between cultural imperialism and a value relativism that leads to all behaviors being acceptable, no matter how shocking they may seem to us, in the name of respect for cultural diversity?

This question is not simply one for the great debates on democracy and human rights. At a more down-to-earth but no less insistent level, it also arises on a daily basis in the subsidiaries of global enterprises.

These companies quite naturally tend to disseminate their own concept of management, along with the corresponding notions of authority, cooperation, conflict management, and professional duty that prevail in the parent company. In doing so, they encounter a diversity of local views on how people should work together, and many of them are wondering what course to follow. Should they, and can they, try to impose their ways of operating and their values without worrying about the risk of creating a "culture clash" that would reduce their efforts to nothing? Or should they instead favor a policy of cultural respect that is likely to mobilize all of their employees and thus lead to greater efficiency? Or is the best option to attempt to reconcile the best of both worlds, which then raises the question of what this implies in practical terms?

On top of this, when Western parent companies have subsidiaries in Southern countries, there arises a moral and political question. Are these subsidiaries the agents of a neo-colonial arrogance that not only undermines the host societies but also destroys their cultures and exploits their wealth? Or are they, on the contrary, vectors of economic, social, political, and cultural modernization?

These questions are particularly visible in the growing number of global companies that adopt various forms of value statements ("codes of conduct," "principles of action," "codes of ethics," etc.) and use these as a basis for developing a "corporate culture" that transcends borders. These codes are necessarily marked by the way in which humankind and society are conceived in the cultures of origin. Can attempts to forge these into a common credo prove both efficient and respectful of local realities? To what extent and in what way can they become accepted and be translated into concrete terms in different regions of the world?

For my part, I have often come across these questions during my research in the foreign subsidiaries of multinational companies. This research is part of an overall program studying how national cultures influence both the way companies function and their management practices (the program content and particularly its theoretical and methodological directions are described in the Appendix). I was given the opportunity to explore this field in greater depth through my collaborative work with the Lafarge Group, the world leader in construction materials. The Group grew out of a company founded in the nineteenth century in France and which now owns subsidiaries in over seventy countries on every continent, with a particularly large presence in the United States and China. It combines the imprint of a humanist tradition and a sharp attentiveness to the international dimension of its management. While it is keen to uphold its values whatever the host culture, Lafarge is only too aware of the need to take root in local cultures. The internationalization of the Group, and particularly the growing presence of Anglophone staff, led to a realignment of the Group's management style in the early 2000s so as to bring it more into step with Anglo-Saxon practices. A major initiative was launched to disseminate across all the Group's business units a "management philosophy" underpinned by a set of corporate values.[1] What was the concrete impact of such a move likely to be? Beyond official discourse, how might this move affect operations in the four corners of the planet? The Group began to wonder. At its request, I carried out a series of investigations[2] to help answer these questions. This led me to take a close look at the many issues involved when this type of approach is implemented, be it in terms of efficiency, of under-lying moral and strategic issues or of understanding the nature of the relationship between values and a particular culture. The purpose of this book is to present the findings of our observations and analyses.

Subjects such as this are most often approached with the implicit assumption that a culture can be assimilated to a set of values. People commonly speak of "Asian values," or of the opposition between the "modern values" specific to the West and the "traditional values" predominant in the rest of the world, or again of a "war of values." In this representation, what a foreign company has to offer can only be implemented by overcoming local values and the resistances they spawn. The implicit benchmark is the light of reason that vanquishes and drives back the darkness of prejudice. It is within this representation that the typical questions on the role of the West, and especially Western businesses, take on meaning. Companies are supposed to choose between a conquering approach that leads them to impose their own values and a respectful attitude that, on the contrary, encourages them to consider each culture as being entitled to keep its own values.

Our observations in the countries for which we analyzed the reactions of the local employees to Lafarge's initiative showed us the extent to which this vision is grossly inadequate.

The Group did not forcibly overturn local values, and would have failed to do so had it tried. In fact, we found a broad commonality between the values espoused by the subsidiaries' employees and drawn from within their own culture and the values endorsed by the Group. This is especially true when it comes to the action of a "good power" that shows a strong sense of justice and concern for those under its authority. Of course, important cultural differences do exist in this domain, but they do not involve values. They are more linked to the way in which values are likely to materialize: the concrete characteristics of a "good power," the way in which superiors create close ties with their troops, precise criteria guaranteeing equal treatment for all, etc. At the same time, when corporate values clash with those embraced by its employees, the latter do not change their convictions. Such is the case with the typically Western values that advocate the freedom to criticize and to openly express differences of opinion.

Is this to say that the specific culture of the Group has had no impact on its subsidiaries? That the Group has simply shown passive respect for the local cultures? This is far from being the case. However, the role it has chosen has little to do with imposing new values. Instead, it has opted to implement values that are already present on the ground. That certain values are present in a society is one thing; whether these same values actually inspire the actions of those in power, be they business leaders or political leaders, is another matter. In both China and Jordan— two countries of particular interest for us—usual businesses practices seem to draw little inspiration from the values underpinning the action of a "good power." In this type of situation, a foreign group that sets store by such values and endeavors to translate them into action—with, of course, the relativity inherent to all human effort—can have a substantial impact if it taps into the previously unexploited potential of culture. Over and above the case we studied, Western firms with a humanistic orientation may well have a key role to play in many parts of the globe where there are high, although often vain, hopes for a strong and just power concerned for the well-being of those under its authority.

All the aspects of Lafarge's approach are highly instructive, be it the written statements of the values the Group wishes to promote or the opinions gathered from employees concerning the Group's management initiatives.

Two reference versions of the Lafarge Group's *Principles of Action* were authored, one French and the other American, with a strong commitment to having them match as closely as possible. On comparing these (Chapter 1), we see that whenever it is a matter of the form that interpersonal relationships take, be it with customers, stockholders, or employees, we exit the realm of those values likely to transcend cultures. Here, there is no escaping the diversity of views on what constitutes the right way of living together. And this relativity is found even within Western societies.

In Chapters 2 and 3, we go on to examine the employees' responses in the Group's Chinese and Jordanian subsidiaries to questions about the influence of the Group's actions on people's work life. In both cases, we identify what distinguishes the local vision of the exercise of power and see how the Group's approach became meaningful and gained acceptance.

Chapter 4 deals with the responses from employees across all the subsidiaries to a survey designed to test people's reactions to the Group's management practices. One particularly striking result of the survey concerns the French. This national category stands out for its skepticism towards any corporate initiative to communicate values. In contexts where subordinates come from the four corners of the globe, French managers need to be aware that the world is not made in their image and that elsewhere, especially in Asia, expectations as regards the ways in which values are diffused can be critical.

The final chapter takes stock of these observations and analyses. Going beyond the area of management, it evokes the role played by cultural diversity for life in today's world. It advocates that a distinction be made between two versions of democracy. On the one hand is a version that could be qualified as restrictive and associated with the exercise of "good power"; this version implies equality before the law, the willingness of leaders to listen to people, and a use of power that is reasonably respectful of the public good, but it also leaves little room for freedom of thought or critical debate. On the other hand, there is a radical version of democracy that goes further than simply exercising "good power," in which freedom of thought and critical debate are fundamental. The first of these versions rests upon values that are seemingly universal. The second, on the contrary, seems to be tightly linked to a conception of societal life that does not easily take root outside the Western world.

Notes

1 *Leader for Tomorrow*, no. 1, August 2003, Lafarge.
2 With the collaboration of Geneviève Felten, Jean-Pierre Segal, Héla Yousfi, and Mingming Duan.

1 France and the United States

Two sets for a single scene

Two reference versions of the Group's *Principles of Action*, one French and one American, were written concurrently by the same authors.[1] They are strictly matched, sentence for sentence. They affirm the same values and, given the proximity of the two languages, often employ the same words (e.g. satisfaction, *satisfaction*; environment, *environnement*; etc.). A cursory reading might well give the impression that the resulting text transcends the diversity of cultures.

Yet, on closer examination, a good many differences appear. And these owe nothing to chance. The text does not simply make mention of values, it also deals with them in concrete terms and describes the relationships that the Group wishes to establish with its customers, its shareholders, and its employees. It does not just state that these relationships must be good, but also places them in a concrete setting and describes the behaviors that the Group as an entity wishes to comply with and those expected from its employees. Yet by entering into concrete realities, the text cannot sidestep the different understandings, on the one hand in France and on the other in the United States, of what makes for good relationships between a company and those involved in its actions. And these conceptions are linked to broader visions, American on one side and French on the other, of what living together means (Box 1.1).[2]

The conceptions involved are apparent in the choice of words and expressions used to describe the various relationships; thus we are not dealing with the same type of relationship if we affirm that we want (or even demand) someone to do something or if we say that we wish (or expect) them to do it. If we pay attention overall to the precise way in which the two versions describe the Group's actions, as well as to the images used to convey these, we see that each version bears the imprint of a culture, the latter being understood as a way of living and working together in harmony. What is involved here are the different ways in which each version of the *Principles* sets the scene regarding the Group's relationships with both the outside world and its employees.

The company as part of society

In the American vision, the role played by business organizations in society is twofold. A company is unequivocally an economic actor that strives for prosperity by satisfying the demands of its customers and shareholders as best it can. It is also part of a community to which it is accountable with regard to its moral stance and its actions at the service of the common good. This vision is often presented by French proponents of societal "modernization" as a model to be emulated. Yet, it has failed to gain much foothold in French thinking, whether in its overtly mercantile aspect or its community-related dimension, both of which arouse a great deal of reticence. It tends to be seen as the coupling of mercenary activity and enlistment into some moral order. A different vision prevails in France, in which one's sense of duty is directly linked to one's duty to oneself and to the rank one holds. These visions pull the two versions of the *Principles* in opposite directions. In the French version, the reticence towards both the mercantile vision of a company and the vision of integration into a community is often apparent. And, at the same time, we also find reference to the commitments that a business organization makes of its own free will to society.

The Group, its customers, and its shareholders

In both reference versions of the *Principles*, the Group emphasizes the importance it gives to its customers and its determination to ensure them satisfaction. Yet, the conception of relations between a company and its customers in each version is not the same.

To take two passages referring to these relations: "*Provide* the construction industry"/"offrir *au secteur de la construction*" ("*Offer* the construction industry"); "*delivering* the . . . products . . ."/"proposer *les produits* . . ." ("*Proposing* products . . ."). Linguistically, it would have been easy enough to write in French "*fournir*" (provide) rather than "*offrir*" in the first case, and "*livrer*" (deliver) rather than "*proposer*" in the second. But this would have profoundly modified the way in which the relations between the company and its customers are framed.

"Provide" and "delivering" set the stage for a commercial relationship between a payer (the customer) who places an order and a provider (the company) who supplies the product ordered. This representation describes a type of relationship that is fundamentally positive in the American view: a contractual relationship between autonomous individuals with converging interests. Conversely, the French equivalents "*fournir*" and "*livrer*," which directly match the terms used in the American version, evoke for the French a mercantile activity of doubtful

Box 1.1 Two conceptions of life in society

In the United States and France, we find two conceptions of society that are substantially different (d'Iribarne, 1989, 2006, 2008). American society has been lastingly marked by the fear of seeing one's fate governed by others. The term "encroach" (defined by Webster's as "to trespass or intrude") well reflects what is at stake. A response to this fear is provided by the importance of contractual relations in society. These relationships bind entities whose rights and obligations are defined with utmost precision by a commitment agreed to by both parties. If I am bound to someone else by contractual ties, they cannot impose anything on me given that they can only require of me what I have consented to in ratifying the contract binding us. Insofar as my consent was genuinely of my own free will, the fear of not having control over my own destiny is thus averted. In business organizations, a meticulous division of responsibilities leading to fixed individual objectives negotiated with one's manager is one of the structuring elements of such contractual relationships. This is also the case for a company's internal regulations, which define in minute detail a set of rights and responsibilities. This contractual approach dovetails with the conception of a local community, particularly a business organization, as a moral community. These two conceptions coexist harmoniously within a vision that considers society as being united around moral values, the observance of which testifies to an individual's credibility and thus contributes to his or her success in the world.

French society, by contrast, is characterized by a different apprehension: that of being forced to bow down, either through fear or self-interest, to someone with the power to harm or bestow favors on you, which is perceived as abject behavior both in one's own and others' eyes. It is humiliating to submit to individuals who for some reason or other (for example, their position as manager or customer) are in a position to confer on you some kind of advantage providing you abide by their demands. In companies, authority relationships and customer relationships tend to be organized, and verbally expressed, so as to keep this image of submission at bay. The reference to the notion of *métier*,[3] to the skilled professional, to the grandeur of one's *métier*, with its concomitant rights and duties, plays a decisive role here. But, while submission is humiliating, it is not the case when an individual freely gives allegiance to an entity (person, cause, institution or even a firm) whose greatness is recognized and with whom they join forces to brave the world.

repute. "*Offrir*" and "*proposer*" imply another kind of relationship that is less self-interested and thus more honorable.

Of course, this does not mean that the company offers or proposes its products in the sense of giving them away. It is clearly understood that the company is offering them in return for money. And yet, the terms "offer" and "propose" are not completely false. What is being offered is no ordinary product, but rather "*les produits, systèmes et solutions les plus fiables, les plus innovants et les plus économiques*" ("products, systems, and solutions that are the most reliable, innovative, and cost-effective"). The company does not simply deliver these products, as would be the case for an off-the-shelf product; it also designs them, brings them into existence and makes them available to potential users. And it is, in fact, true that their existence is in some way "offered." The terms "offer" and "propose" shift attention away from the final and less noble phase of selling the products and onto their design phase—a phase that clearly involves the love of one's art in all its gratuitous dimensions, which thus precludes any assimilation to a subservient activity.[4]

At the same time, where the Group is seemingly subject to its customers' expectations in the American version, the French version presents it as having the power to determine its relationship with customers. This aspect is illustrated by the following comparisons: "*Being* a customer-*driven* organization"/"Orienter *notre organisation vers le client*" ("*Direct* our organization towards the customer"); "*Being measured* by our customer's satisfaction and loyalty"/"Faire *du niveau de satisfaction de nos clients et de leur fidélité* la mesure *de notre success*" ("*Make* our customers' satisfaction and loyalty *the measure* of our success"). In the American version, the customer is the engine and the company is "driven" by the customer's wishes. Its value depends on how it is viewed and treated by its customers; the company can do no more than acknowledge that customer reactions serve as the yardstick to "measure" its worth. This view seems perfectly acceptable in a society where working for other people is taken for granted, where meeting their expectations is what matters and where it is up to the market, through fair competition, to decide what a company is worth.

From a French perspective, passively following customers or being at their beck and call seems to lack dignity. However, freely deciding to "direct" the company towards the customer through a somewhat sovereign approach that allows it to keep the initiative is compatible with a dignified relationship in which concern for customers means taking care of them. Likewise, it is perfectly honorable to freely decide that, since the company has an interest in what the customer feels, it will "make" this into a guiding principle for its actions.

The same contrast between the two versions appears regarding the relations with shareholders: "*Delivering* the value creation that our shareholders expect"/"Répondre *aux attentes de création de valeur de nos actionnaires*" ("*Respond* to our shareholders' expectations of value creation"). In the American version, the company again positions itself unequivocally as a supplier fulfilling ("delivering") an order. In the French version, however, the linkage has been framed differently. It is more a question of the company's sensitivity to a request to which it will "respond," which implies a much greater leeway for action and initiative than simply "delivering." Engaging in a dialogue effectively implies a different type of relationship to that of executing an order. The fact that the company is to a large degree subordinated to its shareholders is thus veiled over.

This French sensitivity to a market dimension also emerges when the company speaks about itself. We have only to compare: "With a leadership position in each of our *business* lines"/"*Leaders sur chacun de nos* métiers" ("Leaders in each of our *métiers*") and "Developing . . . other *businesses*"/"*en nous développant . . . dans d'autres* activités" ("Developing ourselves . . . in other *activities*"). Unlike the word "business," which raises the market aspect of company operations, the terms "*métiers*" and "*activités*" focus more on the industrial side, along with the skill and creative ability that this implies. The same opposition is also found when we compare: "our *portfolio*"/"*nos* activités" ("Our *activities*"). "Portfolio" carries a business connotation that is absent from the term "*activités*."

French reticence towards belonging to a community

The French version of the *Principles* shows as much reticence to the image of belonging to a community as to a market-oriented and self-interested image. This reticence is apparent in the way relations with society overall are referred to. The Group positions itself as a wellspring of influence rather than as part of a whole to which it is subordinated.

We can thus compare: "Contributing to building a better world *for our communities*"/"*Contribuer* autour de nous *à la construction d'un monde meilleur*" ("Contributing *around us* to building a better world"). In the American version, the company is portrayed as belonging to an ensemble of communities (connected to the localities where the company operates) and constituting just one of several components within these communities. This membership implies that the company participates in the efforts made by each community to build a better world. In the French version, the notion of membership disappears. The company portrays itself as an autonomous actor surrounded by other and not necessarily interconnected actors revolving "*autour*" (around) it.

This distancing from the notion of community appears in another passage: "Acting as responsible *members of our communities*"/"*Agir en tant que* citoyen *responsible*" ("Acting as a responsible *citizen*"). The term "citizen" suggests the relatively abstract membership of a vast and purely political ensemble and is a far cry from the emotional ties that exist in a close-knit group, along with the accompanying social pressures, that the term "community" evokes.

We can also compare: "*Our responsibility is* . . . about *complying with* local and international laws and standards . . .*"/"*Nous nous engageons à respecter *les normes et réglementations locales et internationales* . . .*" ("*We undertake to respect* the local and international laws and standards"). In the American version, the fact that one is accountable (a notion closely associated with the term "responsibility") for legal compliance cannot be challenged. Moreover, "comply"[5] evokes passive observance, or a kind of submission to external demands. In the French version, by declaring that it "undertakes" to do something, the company is affirming to the outside world that it is sovereignly taking the initiative to act in accordance with the law.

The above cited sentence continues with: "Our responsibility is . . . as it is *aligning* our actions *with* our values"/"*Nous nous engageons à . . . et à* traduire *nos valeurs dans nos actes*" ("We undertake to . . . and to *translate* our values in our acts"). The idea of aligning one's actions, albeit with one's own values, sounds bad from the French perspective, as it suggests the follow-my-leader attitude of simply tagging along. The idea of "translating" values into action lays greater emphasis on the initiative of the speaker, along with what this implies in terms of free will and the ability to interpret and create.

The same divergence is found in a passage on the company's actions towards its employees. "We *are committed to* helping them"/"*Nous nous engageons à les aider*" ("*We undertake* to help them"). The word "committed" has a slight connotation of submitting to a will other than your own, a will that has given you instructions or set you a task.[6] In the French version, "*Nous nous engageons*" ("we undertake") again suggests a totally independent decision whereby you yourself set, and affirm to the world, the direction you will take.

Human weakness, the religious ethic, and the ethic of honor

Where the American version of the *Principles* talks of striving or doing one's best to perform well, the French version simply states that

improvements are carried out: "*Striving to* continuously improve"/
"*Améliorer continuellement*" ("Continuously improve"). The use of the
term "strive"[7] implies the awareness that, despite your best efforts, you
do not always manage to do what you want to do. This awareness is
meaningful from a religious and moral standpoint, which is ubiquitous
in American culture (Troeltsch, 1958 [1912]; Weber, 2002 [1920]). It
sits well to acknowledge your weakness to the community, much like
the sinner within the church community in the Protestant faiths, which
played a leading role in the founding of the American nation; as Saint
Paul said in the Epistle of the Romans, "to will is present with me; but
how to perform that which is good I find not. For the good that I would
I do not: but the evil which I would not, that I do" (Romans 7: 18–19).
In France, a more secular vision of honor prevails, in which an
individual's weakness is their own affair and does not have to be
acknowledged to the community—a view that prompts people to assert
that who they are coincides with who they claim to be.[8]

The notion of greatness, which implicitly runs throughout the French
version, is sometimes worded quite candidly: "*This leadership*
position"/"notre *position de* leader mondial" ("*Our* position as *global*
leader"). The American wording evokes a competitive advantage within
a business sector. The French version, by contrast, refers to "our position"
and not merely "this position," and further amplifies this leadership
ranking by adding "global," which is absent from the American version.

The company and its employees

The framing of the relations between the company and its employees
reflects the same opposition between two visions of how best to live and
work together as is found in the relations between the company and the
outside world.

On the American side, each employee is individually tied to the
company by a contractual relationship that precisely defines his or her
rights and duties. As such, the employee is regarded as a sort of supplier
who has the obligation to meet the company's requirements, just as the
company meets its customers' requirements. Moreover, all employees
are seen as forming a moral community—a notion conveyed by the
expression "our people"—sharing common values. Through their
contractual ties with the company, each is individually bound to respect
the obligations arising from the values held by the community as a whole.

On the French side, the model of integration into a company takes a
different form. The company is prepared to grant its employees a type
of proud autonomy, much like the independence it is itself keen to

maintain vis-à-vis its entourage. This integration is rarely analyzed in management theories or contemporary sociology. It involves a sort of modern reinterpretation of the olden ties of noble allegiance, a relationship that, in ancient France, represented the form of subordination judged compatible with the status of a free man. This type of relationship rejects all mercenary activity, irrespective of the clarity of the contract governing it. Likewise, it refuses enlistment into a community. However, the relationship carries with it an overall obligation of loyalty and support to one's company, it being up to each employee to decide for themselves on the modalities of this obligation. This relationship with the company is very different from the one evoked by the terms "employee" and "our people." The term *"collaborateurs"* ("collaborators") used in the French version expresses this notion of support that each employee gives to help the company succeed in the missions it has set itself.

The attitude to obligations and particularly rules set by the company

When it comes to the employees' obligations, the American version goes directly to the point: it is clearly stated that each employee must apply the rules set by the company. These directives are part of a contractual relationship and it is taken for granted that they are to be respected, as must all contractual elements. For its part, the company is required to precisely define the obligations incumbent on those who work for it. Throughout the French version, however, this aspect is handled with kid gloves and framed more in terms of some sort of voluntary consent. The reason for this is that from a French perspective, obligation is only perceived as truly justifiable when it stems from what each individual feels are the duties tied to their position in the company—duties regarding which each tends to consider they are the sole judge. In these circumstances, the company can invite, suggest, propose, encourage, but cannot easily presume to impose.

In some cases, an obligation is softened by moving from a wording that firmly expresses the company's will to a formulation giving much more scope to an individual's free agency: "*We want* all of our employees to be key players in the formulation of their own personal objective"/ "Nous attendons *de chaque collaborateur qu'il joue un rôle déterminant dans l'élaboration de ses propres objectifs*" ("We *expect* each of our collaborators to play a decisive role in determining their own objectives"). "Every employee is *expected* to demonstrate commitment to these values"/"*Chacun d'entre nous est* invité *à démontrer son engagement à ces valeurs*" ("Each of us is *invited* to show their commitment to these values"). The French expressions "we expect" and "is invited" are distinctly less imperative than "we want" and "is expected."

Moreover, in the French version, the rules need to be "accepted," a notion that is absent from the American version: "These rules should be *known* by everyone in our organization *and implemented* consistently"/ "*Ces règles doivent être* connues, acceptées et appliquées *de façon cohérente*" ("These rules should be *known, accepted and implemented* consistently"). When individuals deem that they can to a large extent decide on which rules they are duty-bound to observe, they will be highly reticent to implement rules set by the company if they have not already accepted these.

The notion of obligation is also kept at bay by the references not to what a person must do, but to what they must know how to do. "Managers are expected to . . . *delegate* authority"/"*Nous attendons de nos responsables . . . qu'ils* sachent déléguer" ("We expect those in positions of responsibility . . . to *know how to delegate*"). "We expect our people to *share* their experience and to seek those of others"/"*Nous attendons de nos collaborateurs qu'ils* sachent partager *leurs expériences et s'enrichir de celles des autres*" ("We expect our collaborators *to know how to share* their experience and learn from those of others"). What one "knows" how to do is a matter of skill, which leaves a wide margin of interpretation as to how one turns power into action depending on the circumstances rather than on an obligation.

Occasionally, the wording diverges quite substantially: "We want to promote an environment where individuals and teams: *seek* to constructively challenge and be challenged"/"*Nous voulons promouvoir un environnement au sein duquel chaque personne, chaque équipe* pourra*: mettre en cause et* accepter *d'être remis en cause dans un esprit constructif*" ("We want to promote an environment where each individual, each team *can*: challenge and *agree* to be challenged in a constructive spirit"). In the American version, it is quite simply a matter of what each employee will do. In the French version, it is more a question of what they "can" do, or even what they can "agree" to do, if they accept. This is totally at odds with any idea of obligation.

Another way of euphemizing the pressure put on employees to comply with the company's will is to leave those who are subordinated to this will in vague terms. "These rules should be known *by everyone* in our organization"/"*Ces règles doivent être connues* au sein du groupe" ("These rules must be known *inside the group*"). In the American version, each employee is clearly involved with there being no possibility of anyone avoiding compliance. In the French version, the vision is somewhat hazier; it seemingly suffices for the rules to be generally known, which does not preclude some employees from having only a very rough idea of them.

The French reserve towards the American vision of community and morality

In the American world, a shared sense of belonging to a moral community is seen as going hand in hand with converging interests in market-based relationships. In the French world, this community dimension is no better viewed than the market dimension. Thus, whenever the American version of the *Principles of Action* refers to the individual's integration into a moral community, this aspect is downplayed in the French version.

Some American expressions implying a community commitment are replaced in the French version by terms with no allusion to this dimension. "The main process *involving* all levels of our organization is our Management Cycle"/"*Le cycle de management est le principal processus sur lequel* s'appuient *tous les niveaux de notre organisation*" ("The management cycle is the main process *used as a basis* for all levels of our organization"). "*Sharing* systems and tools"/"*S'appuyer sur des systèmes et des outils fiables*" ("*Using as a basis* reliable systems and tools"). Individuals are not presented as being caught up in a collective mode of functioning that transcends them ("involving," "sharing"), but as using, each at their own discretion ("*s'appuyant sur*" ["using as a basis"]), the means of action made available to them.

Even when it comes to relations involving a community-based logic (of help, sharing), the French version steers clear of this in the way it refers to those concerned. "They help *their people*"/"*Ils aident* ceux" ("They help *those*"). "We want to share *our* vision"/"*Nous voulons partager* cette *vision*" ("We want to share *this* vision"). The possessive markers ("their" people, "our" vision) evoking membership of a community are omitted. The reference is to indeterminate individuals, with no mention of belonging ("*ceux*" ["those"]), and what is shared is not specific to a group of people ("our vision") but totally disassociated from the notion of group ("*cette vision*" ["this vision"]).

In addition, in the American version, there is no lack of terms highlighting the individual's innermost feelings ("concern," "good will," "dedication"). The French version tends to replace these with terms ("*priorité*," "*engagement*," "*ténacité*" ["priority," "commitment," "tenacity"]) that on the contrary evoke behavior that can be apprehended from an external perspective, while remaining vague about the individual's inner self. *"Concern* for the group interests"/"Priorité *donnée aux intérêts du groupe"* (*"Priority* given to the Group's interests"). *"Good will"*/"Engagement *personnel"* (*"Personal commitment"*). *"Dedication"*/"ténacité" (*"Tenacity"*). Whereas "concern" elicits a feeling towards something that transcends the individual, "priority" hinges more on behavior where an individual positions himself or herself as an acting subject. The same type of opposition is found in the two other examples.

In the same vein, whereas the American leadership is framed as having the ability to influence a person's inner life ("inspire"), French leadership operates on a more external level (*"fédérer"* ["unite"]). "Leadership is the ability to mobilize people and *inspire* them"/*"Le leadership, c'est la capacité à mobiliser et à* fédérer *des équips"* ("Leadership is the ability to mobilize and *unite* teams"). Similarly, the term "duty," which has moral connotations, is replaced in the French text by the more externally oriented term "responsibilities": "One of the main *duties"*/*"Une des principales* responsabilités" ("One of the main *responsibilities"*).

Whenever the American version refers to personal weaknesses, which are seen as being of sufficient concern to the community to warrant the latter's intervention, the French version redirects focus away from the person and onto the objective situation: "They [managers] help their people deal with *potential performance issues* early on"/*"Ils* [our managers] *aident ceux qui font face à des* difficulties" ("They [our managers] help those facing *difficulties"*). "Willing to ask for help *when they need* it"/*"Demander de l'aide* quand c'est nécessaire" ("Ask for help *when necessary"*). In the French version, it is no longer a question of the inadequacies of an employee that has "performance issues" but of the tough environment they are facing: the "difficulties" they find themselves up against. Likewise, it is not the individual that needs help ("they need") but the objective situation that requires intervention ("when necessary").

When personal weaknesses are nonetheless mentioned, these are depersonalized in much the same way as when a community-based logic is present: "To compensate *our* weaknesses and shortcomings"/*"compenser* les *faiblesses et* les *lacunes"* ("To compensate *the* weaknesses and *the* shortcomings"). The wording "our weaknesses" attributes these to a subject who publicly admits to his or her limits, whereas "the weaknesses" is unrelated to any specific individual.

Much in the same way as when the company frames itself as an entity, the American reference to its employees doing their best with no certainty as to the result is replaced in the French version by a vision where the individual accomplishes what they set out to do: "Focus their energy on . . . *drive for* results"/"*Concentrer son énergie sur* . . . l'obtention *de résultat*s" ("Focus one's energy . . . on *obtaining* results"). Here again, the American reference to individual efforts made and trouble taken ("drive" here in the sense of "energy" or "push") is meaningful from a moral standpoint where doing one's best has a value, but sits ill with a view that privileges the dimension of honor.

A noble allegiance

The type of integration framed in the French version of the *Principles* relates to a form of proud and freely consented noble allegiance to someone or something that surpasses the individual.

The idea of a "mission" is mentioned where, in the American version, it is more prosaically a matter of practical execution: "Focus their energy on *implementation*"/"*Concentrer son énergie sur* l'exécution de sa mission" ("Focus one's energy on *carrying out one's mission*"). Here, we are in another world. Each individual activity takes on full sense within an overall "mission" linked to the position one holds in the company. The primary focus is on the mission rather than on what tends to be seen, from a French perspective, as merely the combined sum of details to be executed. Insofar as a person is true to their mission, it seems only natural to dispose of a broad margin of maneuver regarding the details of how the mission is to be accomplished. Each employee's commitment to their work is not seen as being necessarily weaker than in the United States, but rather of a different nature.

To take a passage referring to each employee's role in improving company performance: "*Resulting from the actions* of all"/"Compter sur *tous*" ("*Counting on* everyone"). This time, it is the French version that sets the stage for a relationship between the company and its employees, whereas the American version is content to describe a physical process that aggregates efficient actions ("Resulting from the actions"). In the French version, the company can "count on" its employees, who will not fail to support its combats.

This type of relationship appears in another passage: "We want to involve all of our people in our ambition and strategies so they can . . . *support the* accelerating *need* for change *that our businesses require*"/ "*Nous voulons impliquer l'ensemble de nos collaborateurs dans nos ambitions et stratégies afin de* . . . nous assurer de leur soutien face *aux changements permanents* qui s'imposent à nous" ("We want to involve all of our collaborators in our ambition and strategies so as to . . . *be assured of their support in face of* the ongoing changes *confronting us*"). In the American version, the employees are expected to do what is necessary in order to meet the demands of the situation ("*the . . . need . . . that our businesses require*"). The relationship with the company is confined to the register of managing things; everyone acts together in an efficient manner. In the French version, on the contrary, the company is engaged in a sort battle (it is "facing" changes that it has to tackle). As a result, it needs to be assured of its employees' support just as, in olden times, a feudal lord setting out to war ensured he had the support of his vassals. This support is to be expected, but it is all the more necessary for the company to solicit it as the commitment is freely made.

Another instance is: "All of our employees are expected to *perform at their full potential*"/"*Nous attendons de nos collaborateurs qu'ils* donnent le meilleur d'eux-mêmes" ("We expect our collaborators *to give the best of themselves*"). Where, in the American version, it is simply a question of individual performance in terms of efficiency, the French version involves the act of "giving," which has an implicit relational dimension—and not just giving a thing, but giving of oneself and the best of oneself. As for the term "*collaborateurs*" ("collaborators"), this also expresses the same idea of each individual's support to help the company succeed in the tasks it has set itself. This is a very different kind of relationship with the company than those evoked by the terms "employees" or "our people."

This type of French approach is accompanied by the call for a form of morality on a very different note from the American style: "*outperforming* themselves"/"*se dépasser pour réussir*" ("*Surpass themselves in order to succeed*"). It is not simply the result the individual achieves ("outperforming") that counts, but also the steps they take and what they become as a person ("surpass themselves").

This support is reciprocal. The suzerain is responsible for supporting his vassals and, at the same time, calls on their support: "*Giving* our people . . . *the support they need to be successful*"/"*Les assurer* [each of our collaborators] du soutien de l'ensemble de l'organisation ("*Assuring them* [each of our collaborators] *of the support of the entire organization*"). The American version refers to each individual's success in their work and to the input provided by the company, which is responsible for giving them the tools they need to succeed (which in turn benefits the company). In this case, it is a matter of converging interests. The French version takes a different stance. Support is not confined to a specific area (the one needed to succeed), but is all-round and directed at the individual. The relational aspect is brought to the fore by fact that the entity ensuring this support is mentioned ("the entire organization")—whereas the American version remains relatively vague on this point. In addition, this relationship is underscored by the fact that the company is described not just as giving silent support, but as addressing each individual to "assure" them they can count on the company.

The French way of becoming integrated into the company, although different from an American-type approach of a moral community, comes across in various ways as very radical: "The higher the responsibility, the greater the *commitment* to our values must be"/"*Plus nos managers exercent des responsabilités élevées, plus ils doivent* incarner *les valeurs du Groupe*" ("The higher *our managers'* responsibilities, the more they must *embody* the Group's values"). In the American version, the Group's values remain extrinsic to the individual, as something to be respected, which is rendered by the term "commitment." Conversely, in the French version, these values constitute a kind of spirit that needs to be "embodied," implying not only a degree of identification with the company but also some leeway for individual initiative when this spirit needs to translate into concrete action. Moreover, whereas in the American version, the required commitment holds good for all employees, in the French version, it is reserved for managers.[9] This stems from the fact that in the French context, the significance of such commitment depends on the position one holds. For those wielding power, it is a question of loyalty and quite fittingly required of them. It is far more ambivalent for those who are tributary to this power, as it may denote a sort of submissive subordination.

Regarding this integration, and contrary to what is observed overall in the *Principles*, the French version is sometimes more demanding ("we want") than the American version (which goes no further than stating "we expect"): "*We expect* all of our people to practice 'the Lafarge Way' in their daily action"/"Nous voulons *que chacun mette en pratique le 'Lafarge Way' dans ses actions quotidiennes*" ("*We want* everyone to practice the 'Lafarge Way' in their daily action"). In the French version, the "Lafarge Way" is a kind of banner (the expression is not translated into French, which thus underlines its reification). However, as nothing precise is involved, simply a spirit to be adopted, we are in register that precludes contractual obligation, and the American version can only wish rather than demand. By contrast, the French version can be all the more demanding as it is a question of sharing a common attitude, and everyone is thus invited to show their allegiance to the company.

Likely cross-influences

The two versions of *Principles of Action* are each marked by their own cultural setting, but the question also arises as to what extent both have been influenced by the fact that they are two versions of one and the same text. Can an American influence be discerned in the French version and vice versa? Does either of them show traits that would not have been present had we been dealing with a purely American text and a purely French text? Are we in fact dealing with a compromise text? To fully answer these questions, the *Principles* would need to be compared to corpora of monocultural texts (which in the French case is problematic, given the American influence in this domain). However, some answers can be conjectured even in the absence of such comparisons.

What appears evident is the neutralizing influence of a censoring effect that avoids wordings too overtly American or French. Each text sets the stage so as to encompass its own view of living in society, but this is only achieved through a relatively discreet modulation of relatively neutral wording.

As a result, the French view of societal life is not expressed in the French version in such clear-cut terms as those found in other corporate codes of conduct that are more rooted in a purely French vision. Thus, in its document, *Les valeurs du groupe*, Suez Lyonnaise des Eaux uses expressions very directly linked to an awareness of the duty of one's rank: "*Notre place et notre ambition de leader mondial . . . nous obligent à ne pas être seulement des bons professionnels, mais les meilleurs*" ("Our position and ambition as world leader . . . obliges us not simply to be good professionals, but the best"), or again: "*Un engagement que nous prenons vis-à-vis de nos clients et nos actionnaires et, surtout, vis-à-vis de nous-mêmes*" ("A commitment that we make to our customers, our shareholders, and above all to ourselves"). It is overtly "our position and our ambition as world leader," and thus a matter of rank, that are the wellspring of obligation and not a concern for meeting customer expectations. Similarly, the duties that an individual acquiesces to originate less in what they owe to others—be it "customers" or "shareholders"—than in a concern for being worthy of the position they hold ("to ourselves"). This inevitably recalls Montesquieu's (1777) words: "The virtues we are here taught [in monarchies] are less what we owe to others than to ourselves; they are not so much what draws us towards society, as what distinguishes us from our fellow-citizens." It is difficult to envisage how this wording could be acceptable in an American world.

Likewise, in the American version, the expressions depicting an American conception of life in society are not as clear-cut as those used by companies that have adopted American values. One good example of this all-American vision is found in *BP*'s *Business Policies*, following its merger with Amoco: "A good business should be both competitively successful and a force for good." Such close ties between economic success and moral commitment, which are taken for granted in an American setting, would be difficult to express so bluntly in a French context.[10]

Nonetheless, these two distinct visions remain perfectly recognizable, since each version bears a strong enough imprint of its context-specific conception of man and society (American on the one hand and French on the other) within which it takes on meaning.

Conclusion

The differences between the American and French versions of the same text well illustrate the processes that come into play whenever it is a matter of concretely expressing values in a specific country.

As soon as the aim goes further than simply dealing with values at a very high level of abstraction, and instead addresses how things can be organized so that these values lead to action, the relationships between the various actors involved (in this case, the company, its customers, shareholders, employees) need to be taken into account. Yet, how these relationships are understood is part of an overall vision of humanity and society that is eminently cultural. Thus, in the United States, a market-oriented image of life in society dovetails with a community-based image. Both these images, however, arouse considerable reticence in France, where acting in what is judged to be a mercantile way appears to lack nobility and where any notion of belonging to a community is quickly perceived as a form of enlistment. However, living up to the position you hold in society implies that you have freely consented to take on certain duties, under no constraint.

When the authors of the *Principles* were searching, in both contexts, for appropriate-sounding or at least acceptable wordings, they themselves must have been immersed in these visions of humanity and society, and used them as yardsticks for choosing expressions compatible with such visions—which thus run through the whole text. The authors did not systematically lean towards dissimilar wordings. Some wordings apparently suited both versions, in which case a literal translation has been used—for example, "Our objective is to grow at a double-digit annual rate over time"/"*Notre objectif est de maintenir sur la durée un taux de croissance annuel à deux chiffres*" ("Our objective is to maintain a double-digit annual rate of growth over time")—although, strictly speaking, the term "*maintenir*" could be associated with the idea of upholding one's rank, a notion not found in the American formulation. Both of these formulations are neutral enough in themselves to be acceptable to either world of meaning. This neutrality, however, is not the rule: in a text only a few pages long, we came across many differences between the American and French wordings, and these differences systematically tie in with what opposes two views of living in society.

Culture continues to have an impact when it comes to putting the values one wishes to promote into practice, as we shall discover on visiting China and Jordan in the next two chapters. Like in France and the United States, corporate values cannot be put into practice if they remain in their pure state. Here as well, we encounter conceptions of living and working together that are unlikely to be overturned by corporate action. But we shall see that it is not necessary to transform a culture in order to bring about substantial changes in a society. Within circumscribed domains of social life, such as a company, if efforts are made to promote values that are rarely implemented yet not unfamiliar to the surrounding culture, this can produce considerable changes in the concrete realm of daily existence, provided it is done in a way meaningful for the culture concerned.

Notes

1 These *Principles*, which had existed since the late 1970s, were redrafted in the early 2000s, with the cooperation of managers of different nationalities. They have been translated into twenty-nine languages. The French and American versions can be downloaded from the corporate website.
2 Some differences, which we will not go into here, can be explained by purely linguistic factors (Tréguer-Felten, 2009).
3 In French, the word *métier* refers to a field of work or occupation in which one excels. It is similar to, although not as restrictive as, the English term "profession" (translator's note).
4 Generally, in France, relationships with customers are expressed in a particular way, with terms such as "prescribe," "diagnose," "welcome," etc. These frame the relationships within a context of disinterested grandeur rather than mercantile servility. We quote, by way of example, a French engineer working as a salesman in the United States, who had held the same job in France and is responsible for selling steel to industrial customers:

> For our customers, we will have the status of a factory representative: we are the ones who will solve all their problems. With them, I feel a little like a general medical practitioner: I listen to them, they confide in me, then I make a diagnosis. Either I'm able to solve their problem by myself, or I direct them to a specialist, a Group colleague with expert knowledge. In the United States, customers are very pragmatic: it's the result that counts, not how you get there. In France, on the other hand, we give a lot of importance to the elegance of reasoning.
>
> (Usinor Group, 1998)

5 In Webster's "comply" is defined as "to act in accordance with a request, demand, order, rule, etc."

6 In Webster's dictionary, the definition of "commit" is "to give in charge or trust; deliver for safekeeping; consign" and "commit implies the delivery of a person or thing into the charge or keeping of another." The term thus evokes a relationship between two entities, one of which entrusts something to the other, the latter thereby becoming responsible for the thing entrusted. The entity that bears the responsibility, as expressed by the wording "we are committed," is thus presented as in some way being entrusted, even though it is not specified by whom.

7 In Webster's, defined as "to make great efforts; try very hard."

8 One of the rules of honor, states (Montesquieu, 1777), is that "when we are raised to a post or preferment, we should never do or permit any thing which may seem to imply that we look upon ourselves as inferior to the rank we hold."

9 One of the authors of the *Principles*, Dominique Hoestlandt, gave us the following explanation for this wording:

> The French prefers to be more explicit. In this way, it responds to a French debate that really did take place (I was present). The question was who would these *Principles* apply to? Should each person believe in them? Defend them? Apply them? Or simply know them to see that they're respected within the Group? It would be inappropriate, in France, to demand that everyone commit to defending and applying such *Principles*. This would be to ignore individual freedom. But we recognize that by making them public and having senior management first and foremost adhere to them, it becomes acceptable, and even honorable . . . so everyone knows what the leaders are committed to. Hence, this unexpected reference to a hierarchical level. But what word should we choose to denote this? Leaders [*Chefs*]? Directors [*Directeurs*]? Bosses [*Patrons*]? Sounds wrong. What about those in charge [*Responsables*]? Too vague, in fact, or too ambiguous: and anyway don't we say that everyone is responsible? All that's left is the paradoxical choice of the word "manager," which is imprecise in French and for this same reason has very few connotations. In English, the formulation would be incomprehensible: why should no one other than line managers be required to observe and apply these principles?
>
> (Personal communication)

10 Moreover, another type of mutual influence is not to be ruled out. In each version, we find "borderline" turns of phrase that do not jar outright, but which are somewhat out of tune with the cultural context, at least in regard to the type of situation in which they are used. Thus the American wording: "Being the preferred supplier for our customers means: best understanding the needs and businesses of our different types of consumers." "Understanding" is of course commonly used in the United States (for example, in the expression "memorandum of understanding"), but in a different context: to agree on the rights of each one. The approach whereby the supplier seeks to understand its customers' needs rather than meet their requirements seems to be inspired by the French vision. Likewise, in "our mission is to provide the construction industry with products, systems, and solutions," the use of "solutions" here seems very French. Similarly, French wordings such as "*nous sommes convaincus que ce sont les résultats qui comptent*" can also be queried. Several

ingredients make this turn of phrase acceptable within a French context; contrary to the American version ("we are convinced that accountability is ultimately about delivering results"), there is no question of accountability. Moreover, the importance of results is underlined by opposing this to the notion of willingness and effort (*"Nous reconnaissons la valeur de l'effort et de l'engagement personnel, mais . . ."* ["We recognize the value of personal effort and commitment, but . . ."]), which fits well with the fact that it is nobler to succeed without making an effort than to make an effort without succeeding. But the use of the term "results" hints at an American influence.

2 China

Between *guanxi* and celestial bureaucracy[1]

When analyzing how the management practices introduced by Lafarge into its Chinese cement division subsidiary (Box 2.1) were received by the local workforce, we came across a question that many companies with Western roots and subsidiaries in China are asking themselves. Such firms seem to be facing a major dilemma: should they adapt to "Chinese" management? Or should they (and can they) pursue practices in line with parent company guidelines? Or again, should they look to implement some sort of synthesis that integrates both Chinese and "Western" practices (with all the ambiguity that the latter implies)? These questions are particularly relevant when it comes to exercising power, as China is a real puzzle for Westerners in this respect. Is it possible to implement management methods, inspired by democratic values, combining a certain balance of power with equality for all? Or would this be meaningless, given that the Chinese are so used to the arbitrary exercise of power and submission from subordinates?

In an attempt to answer these questions, we first examine what seems to be the hard core of Chinese cultural resistance: the exercise of power. Our point of departure is a Western reading of what we encountered in the field, which admittedly amounts to a one-sided perspective. To gain a clearer picture, we take into account the fact that in China the fear that any forthright expression of opinion will degenerate into destructive confrontation plays an important role. This helps us to understand the way in which the company's values translated into reality, and what this meant on a practical level. To conclude, we seek to gain a deeper insight into what we observed, linking our work to various teachings from the Chinese classics.[2]

A Chinese view of power

Many aspects of what we observed tended to reinforce the stereotyped image of a China largely impervious to democratic ideals. Other aspects, however, raised questions as to the appropriateness of this image. This prompted us to try to understand the relationships between leaders and the led from a Chinese perspective, which means that special attention needs to be paid to the risks of openly expressing opposing points of view.

Challenging authority is barely conceivable

A comparison between the Chinese version of the Lafarge Group's *Principles of Action* and the French and American versions (the Chinese translation being based on the latter) shows that the Chinese version reflects a strongly top-down conception of authority. By way of example, we can take the following statements:

- French: "*Les Branches . . . ont un rôle critique à jouer pour* entraîner *les Unités vers une performance accrue*" ("Divisions . . . have a critical role to play in *leading* Business Units towards enhanced performance").
- American: "Divisions . . . have a key role in *challenging* the Business Units to achieve greater performance ambitions."
- Chinese: "Divisions . . . have an important role to play in *setting* performance programs for each Business Unit."

In the French perspective, the role of senior management is to "lead" and, in the American perspective, to "challenge," both of which give subordinates broad leeway for action. From the Chinese perspective, however, it is a matter of "setting programs," which frames the actions of subordinates much more tightly.

This way of operating seems necessary to the parties involved so that each individual knows what they have to do. The interviewees' remarks were expressed in terms of "knowing where we're going," "benchmarks," "the direction" to follow. In the words of one manager, "If we don't have an excellent long-term orientation for our Group, personal objectives are very vague." "With objectives," states an operator, "we know clearly where we're going. I can make them part of my own objectives; the general objectives are reference points for all of us."

This need for benchmarks seems to indicate that the obligation to follow guidelines set by the company is taken for granted: "Since we're in this Group, we must understand and accept its culture," says an operator. "Strict" execution of instructions seems to be considered as appropriate behavior.

A key aspect of the absolute nature of this authority is that open contestation seems barely conceivable. "You can question, of course, but

Box 2.1 A qualitative survey

Lafarge's Chinese cement subsidiary comprises a group of business units with very diverse histories. Our qualitative survey, conducted in 2007, involved three of these. The first, Chinefarge, located in the vicinity of Beijing and formerly a state-owned enterprise, joined the Lafarge Group in 1994. It was with the acquisition of this company that the Group made its entry into China, although not without difficulty. After a long process, it achieved some far-reaching changes in both technical operations and management practices. The second site, in Dujiangyan in Sichuan Province, is a greenfield factory built on the model of Lafarge sites in the more advanced countries. The third, headquartered in Chongqing with two factories in the vicinity (in Nanshan and Guang'an), is a more recent acquisition. Here, the "Lafargization" of management practices is much less advanced. At the time of our survey, management was still very wary and foregrounded the merits of what they described as a "Chinese" approach.

The subsidiary's workforce is almost entirely Chinese. At the time our investigations, the chief executive was French, while the heads of the three business units concerned and nearly all those in positions of responsibility were Chinese.

Forty-six interviews were conducted across different organizational levels, most of them in Chinese with French translation (with the help of Mingming Duan); about ten were held in English or French.

. . . instructions come from above, I can't challenge them," answers one worker when asked what he can do if he disagrees. Certainly, in principle, the "Lafarge culture" has changed things. As one operator states: "Subordinates can directly challenge; that's one of the big differences between Lafarge and state-owned companies." But our interlocutors did not hide the fact that this evolution was little more than one of principle (which doubtless required celebrating out of due respect for authority) that had produced hardly any concrete impact. To the question "Can one question one's superior?," an operator first replies "Yes," then laughs, and to the question "Does this ever happen?" answers "I've never seen it." Similarly, a human resources manager affirms, "If someone doesn't agree, he can speak to his direct boss or to human resources. We can go to the next level in the hierarchy." But he continues: "It's very rare; I've never heard of it happening." In one of the plants, the production manager remarks that "there are ways of pointing out inappropriate behavior by management to an even higher level," but the human resources manager comments: "Disagreements can be reported to higher level management; it's very rare."

We had a first-hand demonstration of just how difficult it is to imagine challenging authority when we discussed the role of the company's *Principles of Action* with our interlocutors. When we asked one plant manager, who was in fact rather critical, whether he could draw on the *Principles* to pull up the subsidiary's managers in the event that they contravened these, he answered emphatically as if our question were preposterous: "No, no, no, I can't."

Yet, some change in this area may well prove possible. A woman manager describes how, when she first joined the company, she regarded the subsidiary's chief executive as representing Lafarge in the highest sense (i.e. embodying the corporate image and values) and thus as an almost sacrosanct figure. As a result, once her superior had decided on something, it was impossible for her to object. She could not understand the French, who saw things differently. Thereafter, she explains, she gradually came to understand that if her superior refused her suggestions, this did not necessarily put an end to the discussion, and could even encourage further reflection. Her perspective thus changed, shifting from an interpretation centered on respect for authority to one focusing on the lessons likely to be gleaned from situations. This manner of seeing things, however, resulted from a highly atypical change in someone who seemed particularly influenced by Western ways.

The weight of this authority goes hand in hand with the severity of sanctions. This seems to go unquestioned. In safety matters, for instance, the only serious criticism we heard of such severity was from an expatriate, who comments: "The approach to safety is disciplinary, punitive." Some of our interlocutors, especially in the units recently taken over by Lafarge, were skeptical about the prospect of change in this area. As one plant manager remarks, "we tried using persuasion for safety issues, but then turned to sanctions, as it wasn't working."

The weight of this authority is also apparent at a more symbolic level. While we were accompanying a manager who had expressed to us his deep concern for the employees, we saw him walk past a female security guard who was standing to perfect attention and totally ignore her military-style salute, as if she were part of the scenery.

If we look no further than the above elements, the conclusion seems clear, and fits nicely with the widespread Western view of China: despite the country's modernization, the Chinese conception of power remains autocratic. This perception concurs with the fact that, at a national level, the transition to democracy does not seem to be a priority and the question of human rights is a thorny issue. Montesquieu's (1777) words come to mind here: "China is therefore a despotic State, whose principle is fear."

The duties incumbent on authority

While many elements reinforce this view of power as a stereotyped image of oriental despotism, other elements are there to ruffle this cliché, since they suggest that authority is by no means exercised in a uniquely arbitrary manner and that, in China as elsewhere, it is marked by duties and limits.

While it is certainly difficult for subordinates to challenge superiors, or even assert themselves too forthrightly, they do enjoy some empowerment with respect to their hierarchy. Mention was made of the fact that, in the company, everyone was given room to express their personal wishes, without however putting themselves in the spotlight. One young woman manager thus described how she went about expressing her wish for greater responsibility (Box 2.2). Clearly, "directly stating" even a "wish" for a higher-level post, let alone the determination to obtain it, is simply not acceptable. But if an employee settles for simply "letting it be known," couching things in terms of "doing more difficult things," "taking on more responsibilities," "working more," or "doing more," the hierarchy "understands." Moreover, management can "consult" the person involved. One operator shows a similar attitude:

> Of course everyone wants to work at the oven. In our yearly appraisal, we're consulted on our objectives for the following year; of course I say "I'd like to". But at the same time, I take training courses, so my skills will be noticed by the manager, and he can see if I'm making progress, if I'm learning the techniques needed to operate the oven.

Here again, the superior "consults" and it is up to him to "notice" and "see" what a subordinate's behavior conveys: "I'm taking training courses," "I'm learning." The operator goes on to say: "It's a two-way dialogue"; "it's a meeting between us." Thus, in some way, subordinates do have their say.

If a superior wants to mobilize his or her troops, or even simply avoid subordinates' departure from the company, which can easily

---

Box 2.2 Letting one's wishes be known

If you make very few mistakes, the hierarchy may think that I could do more; so I was given more responsibilities . . . so, little by little, I'm taking on other tasks . . . So of course I let it be known that I'm ready to assume more responsibilities, to do even more difficult things. My previous manager knew this, of course; when my previous manager handed over to my new manager, maybe they talked about it; the new manager came to see me and consult me on this. Saying directly that I want that job, that particular job, seems pretty aggressive all the same. Chinese people try and get their message across in a subtle way. I'd just like to take on more responsibility. I want to because I'm young, I'm full of enthusiasm, I'd like to work more. The hierarchy understands right away that I'm ready to do more.

(HR supervisor)

---

happen, the superior would be well advised to take into account what is being suggested.

At the same time, the firm assertion of authority, which is well accepted in an American setting, is much less so in China. This is reflected in the Chinese version of the *Principles of Action*, where "we wish" and "we ask" replace the "we want" of the American version: "*We want* all our employees to be key players in the formulation of their own personal objectives."/"*We wish* our employees to play a determining role in formulating personal objectives." "*We want* continuous performance improvement to be a day-to-day priority for each person of our Group."/"*We ask* each employee, as a daily priority, to continuously strive to improve performance."

Moreover, while it is very difficult to challenge superiors, these superiors can take the initiative of engaging in self-criticism to improve their own performance. A human resources supervisor observes: "I had an interview with one of my subordinates, I was doing an assessment with him. I said that I was not doing enough as regards training; this year I will do better."

In any event, superiors cannot make do with managing from the top. They also need to set the example, or otherwise run the risk of finding themselves with a sparse following. According to various managers,

"Managing by example is not the Lafarge way, we have been educated this way"; "If you say things to people and then don't do it . . . this is traditional Chinese culture." Many of them thought it patently obvious that superiors cannot ask of their subordinates what they themselves do not do. "If leaders don't respect the rules, it's impossible for others to do so," says a maintenance worker. "If I don't do overtime, I can't ask others to do it," comments a finance manager. And in the words of a human resources manager, "If the leaders don't implement the performance culture, how do you expect others to do so?"

For many, setting an example implies sharing in a meaningful way the material conditions of those you are leading. As one maintenance worker points out, "You must be with your subordinates." A production manager responds to the question "What does managing by example mean?" by pointing to his smeared work uniform and commenting, "It's plain to see." Several employees speak of the manager who readily mixes with his troops on unpleasant jobs, particularly dirty work or menial tasks: "turning a screwdriver, like the workers," states an operator. "It's a message showing them solidarity, a good example," suggests one manager; "Working on the assembly line is very tough; if I work with them, I can mobilize them to the utmost; I manage to get fantastic results."

The fear of conflict caused by strong self-assertiveness

The restraint expected from subordinates, and in some respects from superiors, fits into a vision of society where pushing oneself too openly to the front is frowned upon, as it carries the implied risk of head-on opposition likely to degenerate into violent clashes.

We find evidence of the concern to avoid such opposition in the Chinese version of the *Principles of Action*, again comparing it with the American text, in the description of what is expected from employees: "Constructively *challenge and be challenged*"/"*Accept and propose* different *ideas* in a constructive spirit." The notion of "*challenge*," with its dimension of interpersonal confrontation, disappears. Relationships remain much more neutral, as people simply "propose" and "accept" ideas. Our interlocutors strongly foregrounded this way of seeing things: "In Chinese culture one of the strengths is to avoid conflict," says a human resources manager. As for a production manager: "We avoid arguments; people discuss beforehand. Everyone has to agree with the decision."

The attachment to well-oiled interpersonal relationships also had an incidence on the course that our own survey took. Our interpreter told us of his discomfort with questions he feared might upset the harmony with the interviewee, and said that he had slightly transformed these when translating to avoid giving a bad impression. One of our questions to a woman manager, which evoked what we viewed as a questionable way of going about things (the earlier mentioned case of the manager who ignored the security guard's salute), prompted her to highlight the value of "saying what must be done, not criticizing others."

Generally speaking, it is considered impolite to push oneself too openly to the forefront. As one operator says, referring to employees who leave the company for more attractive job offers elsewhere:

> When people quit, we don't talk about it; it's taboo and happens behind the scenes. If we have a very, very good relationship, I'll tell you I'm leaving. If someone asks me "You've found an interesting job, a good salary?", I'll reply: "No"; I won't explain in detail.

The interpreter confirmed that is not done to say "I'm leaving because I have a better job than you, I'm more competent," as this would cause others to lose face. Instead, people say: "I've got problems, I can't stand it, I'm not competent." Moreover, putting oneself in the spotlight is risky: "You lose face if you leave and then don't succeed, if you've got to return whereas you said you were going to succeed."

Hierarchical relations become meaningful, as does the whole of existence, within a representation where over-explicit self-assertion is seen as a threat. A case in point would be the remarks cited in Box 2.2: "Saying directly that I want that job, that particular job, seems pretty aggressive all the same." In a Western perspective, individuals are expected to express their desires clearly, but here diplomacy is *de rigueur*: "letting it be known" rather than using explicit assertions, and suggesting that it is a question of "working more," of "doing more," rather than pushing oneself forward. This restraint and, more generally, the absence of open challenges to authority need to be understood as stemming from a concern for harmony rather than as a sign of submission or even, as the first glance of a Western eye would tend to interpret, of voluntary servitude.

The virtues of communicating through hints are not the sole preserve of subordinates, but also concern superiors. In the words of one human resources manager, "In Chinese culture, subordinates obey orders perfectly well; sometimes it's not even necessary to clearly spell out what we want. We only have to allude to something and subordinates understand."

This diplomacy is seen in situations of formal submission that do not imply real obedience. One manager gave an example of how she had handled a difficult situation. Writing to the local authorities, she had ended her letter with a form of address expressed as a request for help and it was impossible to do otherwise without transgressing the code of etiquette. Her expatriate manager, however, took the formula in its literal sense and refused to endorse her apparently submissive attitude. She found it unthinkable to show disrespect towards either of the two authorities, so her solution was to keep the contended formula in the Chinese version, which was sent off as such, and to delete it from the English version sent to her manager. In this way, harmony was preserved between the different parties involved.

Moreover, if you engage in self-criticism with a view to self-improvement, you can criticize others at the same time, since your posture is no longer one of asserting yourself over others. As one woman manager points out: "The Chinese language has one word for to criticize oneself, criticize others, and also look at oneself." Attention thus shifts from the relationship between criticizer and criticized to focus more on the situation and possible actions for self-improvement. The line between the two, however, can be a fine one. For instance, our earlier example of a woman manager who had reacted negatively to our implicitly critical question about the behavior we observed in the company had repercussions on a different level. The following day, the manager in question came to thank us spontaneously in an impromptu meeting for providing her with "feedback" and lessons to be learnt.

When those in authority have a duty to consult and to lend an ear to subtle hints without subordinates having to assert themselves or contest decisions, the hazardous terrain of conflict between antagonistic viewpoints can be circumvented. Even the way of "consulting" is marked by this type of caution. Our interpreter explained that he had used the word "consult" to translate a Chinese term that implies simply wishing to know what the person "consulted" thinks, without eliciting any exchange of opinions.

A just and nurturing order

While the influence of a foreign group is unlikely to revolutionize the references that shape the meaning of hierarchical relationships, there exist vastly different uses of authority compatible with these references. And even though those in authority are deemed to have duties towards the people they lead, nothing inevitably guarantees—in China as elsewhere—that they will fulfill these duties. Undoubtedly, as everywhere else, local practices are very heterogeneous. What Lafarge's influence achieved was to steer these practices within a Chinese universe of possible solutions, but still in line with the Group's values of respect and concern for subordinates. This evolution has had an impact on the style of line relationships and an even more radical effect on the way the company and its managers show concern for what happens to employees. On these points, our interviewees reported a clear break with their previous experiences in other companies, as well as in the state-owned enterprises now under the Group's control.

Consult and set the example

The Group's influence transformed day-to-day line relationships at all levels, including operator level. Measures were taken to give subordinates a voice.

According to one human resources manager, whereas "before, we didn't consult the employees," the practice is now to solicit an employee's opinion before moving them to a different job. One operator points out that this is not merely lip service: "Job vacancies are advertised; if I'm interested, I'll write a letter of application. We take competitive exams, interviews, like people from the outside [laughter]." Mention was made (especially by those who spoke English)[3] of a dialogue between superiors and subordinates as a means of setting employee objectives.

Alongside consultation, a suggestion-giving system was put in place. An operator states:

> Yes, there are channels for getting the message across, to the direct boss of the work unit and higher management. We are assessed on that, we get extra points, five percent of the total; if five proposals are adopted, we get top score.

"We organize meetings to collect proposals; those judged positively carry a reward. First it's discussed at a lower level," remarks a production manager, who nonetheless adds with a smile, "all we do is propose."

There was also a change in the way that superiors set the example. For instance, one operator explains: "The manager helped out with a very dirty operation, he even does tough jobs with the workers; this shows that the principle of managing by example is respected. In the past, managers only ordered people about [laughter]."

A way out of a disorderly world

At the crux of these changes is the way in which the company and its managers show concern for the employees. Going by what we were told, normal operations in both state-owned and private companies in China appear to be characterized by the predominance of short-term considerations, influential networks of interests, and scant regard for employees, particularly with respect to training and advancement prospects. It was largely in contrast to this environment that the Group's way of operating took on meaning.

In the words of one manager: "In state-owned enterprises, performance is not important; what matters is the relationship with your superior, or with important people ... In my department, *guanxi*[4] was more important than actual performance." When describing the normal running of Chinese companies, those we spoke to often underlined the role of relationships with those in power, as opposed to the quality of individual contributions to company operations. "Before, in state-owned companies, it was personal relationships that made things happen, not competence, and only a minority benefited," says an operator. This widespread way of functioning is encouraged by insufficient clarity in assigning responsibilities and the lack of rigor in assessing results. One supervisor explains: "In the past there was no job description; we didn't even know the requirements for a given job position. We didn't know if we were really competent, as promotion happened in an authoritarian manner." "In private companies, there's no evaluation system that measures things in a truly objective way," remarks a supervisor.

This universe, with so few norms, is strongly marked by the reign of self-interest. "Before, personal relationships in state-owned enterprises were very complicated; everyone is out for their personal interest, and doesn't care much about others," recounts a supervisor. According to one operator, "In state-owned enterprises, sometimes people don't hesitate to fake the figures for the managers' personal objectives." "Private companies only look for results; sometimes people don't care about the means of getting there; morally, it's not acceptable," claims an operator.

From favoritism to equal rules for all

Unlike the "ordinary" business world, Lafarge appears to be governed by standards that are both clear and respected. The objectivity made possible by having and effectively implementing rigorous procedures is continually contrasted with *guanxi*, which encourages favoritism. As one manager explains, "Everything is done according to very precise, well designed procedures ... At Lafarge, performance plays a decisive role in determining salaries ... which we very much appreciate." One operator comments, "Here, everything is really genuine, all the figures truly reflect reality … It's clear for everyone what concrete measures need to be taken to reach objectives; everyone looks after their own job."

This focus on performance is a source of pressure that was largely absent from state-owned enterprises, but one that on the whole seems to be well received. As one manager puts it, "Before, there was little pressure, few indicators to measure productivity; an operator could stay in his cabin without checking whether the conveyor belt was moving coal. With precise measurement indicators, he is more motivated to be productive." An operator says, "Of course there's real pressure, but it's positive pressure that motivates you to work; in the state-owned enterprises everyone worked as they liked." Another operator comments: "Compared to state-owned enterprises, Lafarge demands the utmost from everyone; it's the result that counts. Most of us are happy to accept the pressure, a minority can't take it. It's a question of time."

Our interlocutors contrasted what they described as "management by people"—meaning the reign of arbitrary personal decisions and favoritism tied to relational networks—and "management by a system"—meaning strict compliance with a set of rules: "For me, it's the standards, the rules, that make Lafarge work, not individuals." Far from being viewed as a source of dehumanizing bureaucratic impersonality, this formalization was, on the contrary, perceived as a vector for a more human dimension: "If an evaluation system is not objective, people may be judged in a totally random, subjective manner; personally, I find that inhuman. The objectivity of an evaluation system is one of the key ingredients of humane management," says a supervisor. An operator remarks in the same vein: "Before, promotion and personal development very much depended on personal relations; Lafarge puts people first!"

This way of functioning can also tie in with a change in the underpinnings of trust. One manager strongly insisted on the difference between "trust," or in other words a personal trust based on a relational logic, and "confidence," which hinges more closely on a professional logic linked to competence.

To what extent does objectivity, with its recognized virtues, have a real impact on the day-to-day running of the company? One of our questions on whether some degree of favoritism persisted drew a laugh from one operator, who went on to say "there is some, but I've never heard of that sort of thing; the Chinese are reluctant to talk about their feelings with their entourage." But judging from all that was said to us, there is little doubt that the company has definitely left behind the ordinary Chinese business world.

Supporting each individual in their personal development

The place given to each employee's personal development was particularly appreciated. One operator comments, "I learnt [from the *Principles of Action*] that the development of a company depends on the personal development of its employees." "Lafarge attaches great importance to personal development; the atmosphere is favorable to promotion, to taking initiatives."

The aim is to help every employee to develop. One supervisor remarks: "Most importantly: I understand that management attaches great importance to humaneness and is closer to people, to each employee; helps employees to succeed. This particularly struck me." Performance requirements are part of an overall perspective encompassing this kind of support for employees. For one woman manager, objectives should be "difficult but not overly so" with a view to "self-improvement" and, for those who find it hard, "offer more encouragement". An operator remarks:

> Lafarge plays the persuasion card, encouraging people. In the past, there was talk of systematically excluding the weakest people; that's no longer the case now. We are encouraged to progress without worrying about it too much; the fact that someone is not as good, and gets a B or a C, doesn't mean that they work badly, but simply that others work better.

The subject of training was particularly underlined. In the words of one operator, "Personal development; Lafarge provides a lot of training programs, provides support if need be." Contrary to traditional Chinese companies, Lafarge does not reserve training programs for long-serving employees, which is a sign of the confidence it places in new hires.

The corporate safety policies, to which the company has devoted a great deal of effort,[5] are seen in the same light. As one manager puts it, "When someone has an accident, the person suffers greatly, but so does his or her family; we don't want that," adding "this is a real sign of humaneness." These policies seem to epitomize the corporate motto of "making our employees the heart of our company", explains a manager. Formerly, the usual response to accidents followed a logic of group connivance: "Previously, whatever the accident, we didn't look for the cause; we had to show great solidarity," notes a supervisor. The mindset has since shifted to a logic based on an orderly functioning, the observance of rules, and efforts to progress. He continues: "Now, we're ashamed of accidents; we have to find the direct and underlying causes. Before, doing this was frowned upon; now, we think it's a good idea."

A long-term perspective

A reference to the long term, which is absent in the American version, was added to the Chinese *Principles of Action*: "Focusing on performance improvement"/"Focusing on *sustainable* performance improvement"; "an increasing share of the fast-growing markets"/"*sustainably* increasing the share of the fast-growing markets." Personal development ties into this long-term perspective: "If the company has no future, I won't work here; my personal development is linked to the future of the company," says one operator. Conversely, the head of a production department talked at length about an episode involving the departure of a group of operators: "They said at the time, in 2004, that they couldn't see much future; now that Lafarge is moving forward much faster, some have returned."

This is comparable with the opposition, which was present multifariously in our respondents' minds, between opportunistic behavior geared to short-term gain and the construction of a collective order to ensure some degree of permanency.

Complex adaptations can take time

Although the mode of functioning being set up has met with a positive reception overall, not everyone has taken it on board. Among the managers we met, some thought that the fact of formalizing management structure was to blame for slow decision-making in areas where speed is vital. This view was particularly highlighted with respect to the subsidiary's growth (mainly for company takeovers), and more generally to managing relations with customers and the authorities. In these situations, someone who manages by instinct seems more attuned to the way society functions, and thus more efficient, than their counterparts who have to follow a system of rules. According to one plant manager, if the aim is to develop company business:

> two key words, speed and size; we're too slow; we're drowning in figures, losing a lot of opportunities, Lafarge management is very rigid; a lot of initiatives can't be foreseen; we're bridling the initiative of local business units; we have to get rid of unnecessary, bureaucratic tasks; for me the key indicator is profit; if there are too many indicators, we get lost, we lose sight of the essentials; I need much more autonomy, otherwise it's not worth my staying.

One business unit president contrasted Westerners, who manage through formal institutions, with the Chinese, who manage through people. He maintained that although managing through institutions reduces the risk contingent on the personality of individual managers, if they are competent it nonetheless cramps their initiative and slows down company growth. In the Chinese approach, he adds, power is centered on managers. At a more modest level, personal trust between individuals is still very important. As one operator explains:

> With people I don't know well, I need more time to get to know how to communicate and talk with them; for those of us who work at the oven, communication makes the job much easier. We spend a lot of time discussing day-to-day problems; we share our experiences. For one problem, there are many different explanations; some may have found solutions on the Internet or elsewhere, in manuals. We have lots of opportunity to discuss, to play cards as well; we organize meetings.

Customer relations also fall between two stools. When asked about the difficulties likely to be caused by dovetailing Lafarge ethics and market practices, our respondents mentioned the fact that several more or less "clean" markets existed. Even when corruption is no longer an issue, maintaining good customer relations, along with the sometimes necessary flexibility, continues to play a role. In the words of a sales manager,[6] "some things are negotiable in a contract: prices, terms of payment; things that are not written down."

All in all, combating the excesses of a logic based on interpersonal relationships without losing too many of the positive aspects that it brings remains a sensitive issue for managing the company.

Furthermore, it is difficult to connect up a vision of the company as great and nurturing and the way the labor market operates. To what extent can a benevolent power that helps employees to progress set them in competition with people from outside the company? Even when labor market rationale is not openly criticized, it is seen as something imposed rather than recognized as fully legitimate. One production manager, for instance, made some rather disillusioned remarks about operators who had left the company and later returned, sometimes to a higher position than his own: "They skipped several levels; it's normal. It's the market playing its role of adjustment." The operators complain about the level of pay, basing themselves on a logic that is alien to the market. As one business unit president comments: "In the survey carried out after L.F.T.,[7] I remember one response: 'if we really worked for Lafarge, we'd get better pay. Lafarge is rich'; they're not thinking of the market."

The potentiality of a culture

The reactions to the management practices that Lafarge has endeavored to introduce, the resistance encountered, and the successes achieved are all tied to the way in which the targeted changes take on meaning in a Chinese setting.

What is expected from authority?

The distinction between good power and bad power is predominant in Chinese culture. But what characterizes a good power and, even more so, safeguards against corruption and the abuse of power is not a carbon copy of what seems self-evident in Western countries in this domain.

The vision of the virtues of debate and the reasoned confrontation of viewpoints leading to the expectation that enlightenment will spring out of antagonistic ideas, and the agonistic conception of the search for truth associated with this vision are rooted in the Greek experience of the *polis* (Vernant, 1962). It is this legacy that has prevailed in the West and shaped, more particularly, the way in which the meaning of autocratic power as opposed to democratic power has developed. A political regime with no opposition to constantly challenge the actions of those in power is considered to be despotic. Modern China has inherited a different history and another world vision. The opposition between good and bad power has been constructed differently (Jullien with Marchaisse, 2000). There is no "tradition of public debate with arguments for and against, *logos* against *logos*" (Jullien with Marchaisse, 2000: 164).[8] The fear reigns that an overly weak power or vacillating rules will open the gates to disorder, with the danger that society will collapse into anarchy. The Western conception of individual autonomy is deemed disquieting. The strict enforcement of rules is thus seen as necessary, and all the more so as compliance cannot be taken for granted given that everyday relationships are so marked by strong individualism.

At the same time, the opposition between good and bad power lies at the heart of Chinese history as portrayed by the sages (Granet, 1994 [1929]). The representation of a good power is inspired by the image of the good leader devoted to the good of the people and a model of virtue, as described by Confucius (1971 [1893]: 6:22) "To give one's self earnestly to the duties due to men . . . may be called wisdom." The leader exercising power in this spirit is selfless and does not abuse his authority: "the person in authority (*junzi*) . . . pursues what he desires without being covetous . . . is not this to be majestic without being fierce?" (20:2). He sets the example of upright conduct: "If a minister make his own conduct correct, what difficulty will he have in assisting in government? If he cannot rectify himself, what has he to do with rectifying others?" (13:13). The great legendary sovereigns of ancient times are thus portrayed as having lived solely for the good of the people, without giving thought to themselves (Granet, 1994 [1929]). Bad sovereigns, however, are portrayed as driven by a combination of cruelty and pride, unmindful of Virtue, which befits the natural order of things (Granet, 1994 [1929]: 26, 45); the tyranny they wield is depicted as ultimately leading to anarchy (Granet, 1994 [1929]: 53). Obviously, the Chinese are not "Confucians" in the sense that their day-to-day behavior is necessarily inspired by the Master's teachings; in any event, cultural context produces no magical effect on behavior. Yet, Confucius' teachings have helped to construct the interpretative framework used by the Chinese to make sense of daily life and to judge their fellow men. His teachings also reflect and are influenced by a world vision that permeates China's history.

When an individual holding authority fails to create harmony, they lose their legitimacy. In the traditional Chinese view, they have lost their celestial mandate and must be replaced. This is quite different, however, from openly contesting a respected power. Certainly, Chinese tradition has no lack of representations that provide meaningful underpinnings for practices that contrast sharply with the passive respect for authority. Some of these, such as the figure of the sage who enlightens the emperor, if need be by opposing him, were used in the employee *Principles of Action* training. But here one is treading on sensitive ground.

The Chinese classics illustrate the quandary raised by this question. In Confucius' writings, the reference image is that of a perfect order where there is no room for any form of contestation: "When right principles prevail in the kingdom, there will be no discussions among the common people" (Confucius 1971 [1893]: 16:2). Clearly, such exercise of power is not without risk, since the absence of contestation may stem from the lack of opponents, whereas the situation should in fact produce opposition. Confucius (13:15) is aware of this:

> There is, however, a saying which people have—"I have no pleasure in being a prince, but only in that no one can offer any opposition to what I say!" If a ruler's words be good, is it not good that no one oppose them? But if they are not good, and no one opposes them, may there not be expected from this one sentence the ruin of the country?

The survival of the State demands that people be able to express themselves openly before the sovereign: "Tsze-lû asked how a ruler should be served. The Master said 'Do not impose on him, and, moreover, withstand him to his face'" (14:22). But revealing the truth, which is necessary for the public good, is a delicate matter for, unless close ties have been woven between the person exercising power and the person criticizing, the latter's actions may well be seen not as salutary advice, but as a lack of respect; "Tsze-hsiâ said: 'Having obtained the confidence of his prince, one may then remonstrate with him. If he have not gained his confidence, the prince will think that he is vilifying him'" (19:10).

Escaping the logic of guanxi

Chinese civil society functions according to a logic of solidarity networks uniting private interests (*guanxi*). Maintaining order traditionally falls upon a strong political power implemented by a vast administration acting in the name of the "Son of Heaven" (the "celestial bureaucracy") (Balazs, 1988 [1968]) and duty-bound to tend to the people's good. This dual dimension influences what the Chinese employees expect of Lafarge, as well as how its management principles are understood. It is what underlies the opposition between being "managed by men" and being "managed by a system."

State-owned enterprises often used to operate using a network-based logic, and this holds true for privately owned companies. Lafarge is perceived, on the contrary, as leading its employees with a form of strong, just, and nurturing power that matches the ideal image of "celestial bureaucracy." The role of competence, where justice (judge according to competence) is crossed with nurturing (develop competence), and the role of safety seen as protecting not only individuals but also their families fit perfectly well into this picture. The same is true for the importance placed on a long-term perspective. If a "system" can be perceived as giving more place to "humaneness," as being "closer to people, to each employee" than men are, as putting "people at the heart of policies" whereas men do not, this is because the traditional role of a public authority true to its mission is to take action towards these goals.

When the exercise of power changes in this way, individuals remain just as attached to their own interests as when networks of interest and friendship dominate. They expect authority to play a large role in what each derives individually from their own work. If they appreciate the resulting change, it is because they have the feeling of being better off than when each has to protect their interests alone, in a more anarchical world.

Ultimately, this change in the way power is exercised, together with the importance it attaches to setting examples, listening to subordinates, and showing concern for their personal development, has led Lafarge to distance itself radically from the most common practices of Chinese companies. However, this reform was carried out without departing from the framework offered by Chinese culture itself. Its meaning was interpreted in the light of the traditional Chinese image of a good power dedicated to the people's good. Not that this image has always inspired Chinese governance—far from it. But it is present in the collective imagination, ready to give a positive sense to practices in tune with the model it proposes. The shift from a disorderly mode of functioning, where each person's defense of their own interests is limited only by the existence of networks of interest and friendship, to an orderly functioning guaranteed by a just, strong, and nurturing power based on a "system" that applies strict rules does not mean introducing into Chinese society an alien conception of the role of power. Clearly, applying this Chinese conception to the corporate world is far from simple given that it contrasts sharply with the practices most commonly found in Chinese companies, and Lafarge's merits in successfully carrying out this transfer should not be underestimated. But admittedly, no major cultural blockage exists here. However, the possibility of freely contesting authority is indeed alien to the Chinese world and, on this point, the company had little chance of becoming a force for change.

Conclusion

Lafarge has helped to integrate into Chinese management practices values that are by no means unfamiliar to a Chinese environment but which have little impact on the country's everyday business practices: the concern for employees, which is a value particularly dear to Lafarge, the rejection of arbitrariness, and equality of treatment with respect to the rules—all inherited from a set of core values that Western societies also share.[9] The Group's actions to implement a "performance culture" with all this implies in the way of rigorous evaluation and fair remuneration for individual contributions, to invest heavily in training and to give priority to safety have meant that these values were able to change from simple statements of principle into a guide that inspires everyday activity. The very favorable welcome given to this change is commensurate with the gulf between ideals and practice that is usually found in Chinese companies. Lafarge has, at the end of the day, enabled its Chinese employees to take great strides in implementing a Chinese vision of a good power within a corporate setting.

Notes

1   A first version of this chapter appeared in *Gérer et Comprendre*, 2009, no. 96, pp. 4–14.

2   Some of the problems facing the subsidiary's management team, and which still pose a challenge in the more recently acquired business units, are not specific to China. They relate to the way in which state-owned enterprises in China generally operated under a socialist economy. The same traits were found in Eastern European companies. Bertrand Collomb, the Group's CEO at the time of our qualitative survey, comments on Lafarge's arrival in China:

> the first job of the team of expatriates was to establish work and performance requirements in a factory where a hugely overstaffed workforce with over twenty hierarchical levels had developed lethargic habits. Removing the "beds" from offices was one of the symbols of this "disciplinary" action.
>
> (Collomb, 2007: 11)

The management of this transitional phase will not be dealt with in the present volume.

3   One could ask what accounts for the nuances in what was said by interviewees using English and by those using Chinese. One explanation may be that the former were more influenced by Western cultural references than the latter. A second reason, distinct from the first, is the fact that speaking in English tends to lead people to adopt official company discourse, whereas speaking in Chinese leads to greater distance from this (Harzing, 2002).

4   *Guanxi* literally means "relationships" but in the Chinese business world it denotes personalized networks of influence.

5   The arrival of the Group was marked by a spectacular change on this front. In the first plant acquired, for example, the number of hours lost due to accidents was cut twentyfold in the space of three years.

6   In relations between Chinese companies, contract terms are often little respected, and compensation can rarely be obtained through the courts. Consequently, a contract between companies is generally seen as only one episode in a business relationship where receivables and payables balance out over time. The discrepancies between what is set out in a contract and what actually happens as regards deadlines, quality, or payment are to be interpreted in this perspective. The fact of reaching agreement on a specific contract enables the parties to know who is indebted to whom and for how much. This type of functioning is grounded on long-term relationships (Duan, 2007).

7   *Leader for Tomorrow* is the name of the corporate program to renovate management.

8   Original French text: "une tradition d'un débat public argumenté pour et contre, *logos* contre *logos*."

9   It would be beyond the scope of this book to discuss the frontiers of what may be qualified as such, notably in Eastern Europe or in Latin America. We shall use this expression in a restrictive sense, to evoke European societies and their heirs, such as the United States, whose pioneering role in the emergence of modernity and the advent of rule of law is difficult to contest.

3 Unity and tribalism in Jordan

The Middle East is one of the regions of the world where, as in China, the forms of societal organization prevalent in the West, and what is qualified as a Western conception of human rights, are particularly contested. Here also, companies face issues of adapting forms of governance to local settings and this was what we encountered at Lafarge (Box 3.1).

We investigated the ways in which the management methods inspired by the Group's values made sense within the local conceptions of life in society and governance. At the time of our survey, the subsidiary's integration into the Group was much less advanced than in its Chinese counterpart.[1] Furthermore, at that point in time, the transformation process associated with the *Leader for Tomorrow* (L.F.T.) program was in its early days. What transpired above all in our survey were the hopes and apprehensions raised by this process. It is in such situations that it is most useful to be aware of which aspects of foreign group's proposed orientations are either likely or unlikely to be accepted by local personnel, and under what conditions.

We shall first see that a wide gap separates the ideal vision pervading our interviewees' remarks and the worklife experience that they denounce. We then examine the vastly differing reactions to the various managerial measures that the parent company was trying to introduce. In this management approach, everything that evokes the vision of a community united under common ideals and rules, with recognized equality for all members and a benevolent authority to give direction, musters support; by contrast, there is a rejection of anything likely to place individuals in an inferior position, which contravenes the ideal vision, or likely to resemble a worklife they strongly criticize. Lastly, we shall see that our observations gain in insight if we take into account the fact that two largely antagonistic visions of life in society, one tribal and the other religious, characterize the country.

Box 3.1 A survey

The Lafarge cement subsidiary in Jordan was a state-owned enterprise, J.C.F. (Jordan Cement Factories), privatized in 1999. It is headquartered in Amman and has two plants at Fheiss and Rashidiya. It holds a quasi-monopolistic position in its sector. Among the staff, an older generation that inherited the habits of a public-sector bureaucracy with traditional references exists alongside a new generation of executives educated in American or European business schools. At the time of our survey, conducted by Hèla Yousfi[2] in December 2004, an attempt to renovate management was just beginning under the L.F.T. program. At the time, the program had only been presented to the more senior management levels.

Twenty-three interviews were carried out—eleven at headquarters and six in each of the two plants—with staff already briefed on the L.F.T. approach. As this program had only reached a certain level of managers, the interviews did not involve either supervisors or workers. They were conducted in Arabic, English, and more rarely in French (for French expatriates). Unless indicated otherwise, the quotations used are taken from the comments made by Jordanian managers.

A large gap between the ideal of unity and actual experience

Our respondents' comments were marked—to a degree unprecedented in our enquiries—by references to what the ideal functioning of a company should be. The expressions "have to," "must," "should," and "what we are lacking" were used repeatedly. The ideal image serving as the yardstick to judge reality is that of a community governed by rules applying equally to all and united around a guide who is close to those he governs, acts fairly and sets the example. Yet, at the same time, the company is still structured around highly hierarchized social groups whose relationships are somewhat tense, and the influence of personal relationships makes compliance with rules a complicated matter.

A strong aspiration for equal rules for all under accessible and just leadership

Our interlocutors unanimously stated that everyone, whatever their rank, must be answerable to a common rule: "There *must* [our emphasis] be a reference, a reference that governs both you and me. Me as an ordinary worker and you as top management, so ultimately we have the same reference"; "*What we are lacking* are general principles . . . That's what will regulate the relationship between a boss and his subordinate. And this is what *plagues* us at J.C.F., *we have no* uniform standards." Of course, different functions may exist, but within a framework of rules that apply to all. "I should have a manual that states clearly what the department head is authorized to do: 1, 2, 3, 4, and these prerogatives *have to be* clear even for the employee." "The prerogatives and responsibilities for each job position *have to be* specified." "Rules *have to be* established."

Correspondingly, a world lacking rules or clear principles, in which the manager's wishes are law, is rejected: "I don't want the director or supervisor to tell me every day what I must do." "The fact that there aren't any principles means that daily work is based on personal instructions . . . And that creates problems between the boss and the subordinate, because *there aren't any* unified work principles."

This hoped-for equality before the law does not preclude a strong authority wielded by a leader who is a source of security and guiding principles: "It's the boss who ensures protection and stability for his employees just as the king protects his people and, in return, the employees owe him obedience and loyalty [*taa wa walaa*]"; "*We need* strong leadership, *we need* . . . a stable recourse that has authority over everyone and is a decision-making center." The initiative *must* come from the top: "For it to be applied . . . it must begin at the top. I'm a manager . . . I function according to a specific culture; it *must* impact my subordinates in some way or other." A leader extolled in these terms does not however use his rank as a pretext for aloofness: "there *must* be communication between top management and the lowest-level person in the factory hierarchy"; "He *has to be* present on the ground" and not just say "'do this, this, and this.'" A manager is expected to show moral leadership, which enables him to reconcile his elevated position with an emotional closeness: "*We need* a leader who sets a moral example and not a manager: a leader who is at the same time a moral example and a strong and fair decision-maker." This type of leader makes employees feel that he "shares their sorrows and joys," and that he is "with them body and soul."

An experience of distance and arbitrariness

According to those we spoke with, what is valued bears little resemblance to the day-to-day experience of company life.

Many criticized the divide between those who lord it in the offices and those who toil away in the factories, the former never deigning to mix with the latter (Box 3.2). It is not that work relations as such pose a problem: "Technically, our relationship is good, our collaboration is excellent, and if we need them on a technical level, they come." But there are two opposed worlds: the privileged world that is "sitting comfortably" and "doing nothing" and the other, in the factory, that is "making the effort." The first "takes advantage" of the "dust" that the second "eats." The "fatigue" of some "goes to" the "benefit" of others who "take everything" from them. Some enjoy "luxury," "privileges," "big advantages," the possibility of "having everything" "easily": "trips," "training," and so on, while the others have an obligation to "keep count of everything, with cars "in a sorry state." The masters are so far removed from those that serve them that the latter "know nothing of the nature" of the former's work. Here we are at the opposite extreme to the much-desired equality.

This divide between the top and bottom of the hierarchy also makes itself felt in decision-making processes: "There are strategies, parachuted down, already set out and designed and you are only required to apply them, that's all." "They launched a series of projects for reform . . . they didn't ask many employees and factory engineers for their opinion." The distance is so great that not only is consultation with the rank and file inexistent, but no one is even informed: "The decisions came from the top. A lot of people in the factory weren't informed of these projects."

When responsibilities are assigned to the lower levels, they are rarely respected:

> For example, an entrepreneur comes to see me asking me to settle his invoice. So I take a look at what he's done, I do my sums and deduct the work he hasn't done. And later, I'm surprised to discover that he has been paid the full amount.

The hierarchy does not even see fit to inform subordinates of what its actions are based on:

> So, had my boss warned me that it isn't 1, 2, 3 because there's been a change, if he'd explained the situation to me, I would have agreed. But if I do a job, and then realize that someone else has changed things afterwards, then there's a feeling of frustration. Because then

I no longer know what company policy is. I mean I follow a policy . . . and you realize that things get mixed up and you don't know who's the decision-maker in all that.

In these circumstances, "what's my role as an accountant, or controller, what's my role?"

**Box 3.2   Head office management and
the factories**

Disparities exist between general management and the factories and everyone will say as much. When we go down to see management [at head office], we take a factory car; when you see the management's cars, it's luxury; the factory cars, as you see, are in a sorry state. They have everything and we have no services, why? The people here say: "we here eat dust and they over there take advantage of it." There's no equality, and that you can see for yourself.

For them [the workers], it's the worker who tires himself out, who is productive, who brings the money into the company. Whereas the person who is managing is sitting comfortably doing nothing, he doesn't contribute as much as he [the worker] contributes, and management has more privileges than him. Their fatigue goes to the benefit of head office management in Amman. That's what most of the company's employees think. This is why you don't see anyone from head office in the company, very rarely, or when they come, they go as far as this building, they don't go into the factory. Maybe the work they do at head office is important work, grandiose, but people in the factory don't know anything about the management job that the person in Amman is doing. This is sort of frustrating for the employees.

We, individuals, without speaking of myself personally, head office takes everything from us. We tire ourselves out, we make efforts, we try to reform, arrange things, etc.; they have all the big advantages, they get to visit, they get to travel, they get good training courses . . . And added to this are other advantages. For example, [if] I'm a director from general management, I can easily get a car, I can easily get a doctor, I can easily get a school for my children, whereas me, I'm on a site where I have to keep count of everything.

The longing for a well-ordered world, where a person's future does not hinge on someone else's whims but rather on the application of clear-cut rules that are the same for all, is constantly thwarted: "We function according to moods, people's moods, pressures from the unions, [tribal] pressures, government pressures, pressures from the representatives, the representatives of the people, I mean." Favoritism determines not only how someone is assessed but also what they are paid for their contribution: "There is no justice, that's what I feel . . . If you aren't in perfect harmony with your line manager, it's hard to get a good assessment. Despite the fact that you may have good ideas." Even when procedures exist that are supposed to make an objective appraisal possible, their spirit is not respected:

> The appraisal remains subjective, for example, I have ten criteria on the appraisal sheet and each criterion is scored out of ten with the total being one hundred. Me, as a director, if I have to assess you, I say to myself: "I feel like giving you 80," so without looking at the criteria, I'll arrange it so that the total adds up to 80.

This gap between an ideal and reality feeds a desire for radical change: "so you stop and you tell yourself, 'this system, I've had enough, it's over'." What we encountered yet again was the wish that a well-organized world would finally emerge, in which all is as clear as a numbered sequence and each person's situation governed by a respect for fundamental principles: "And I'm going to start with a new system: 1, 2, 3, 4. Its principles are justice, equality, equity between job positions, between people . . ."

But a change of this kind is all the more difficult to bring about as the rigor of a rule-governed world is not really accepted, despite there being an attachment to the principle of change:

> The employee doesn't accept a response in line with the rules, procedures or instructions. He wants there to be exceptions. And if he doesn't get the response he was expecting, he wants to see the decision-maker higher up. If that doesn't satisfy him, he wants to see top management. So that's what our company is like . . . Me, I want such and such, so I must get it, even if I have to go to right to the top of the pyramid.

"The worker is fond of special-case situations, he doesn't just implement a decision. He'll always try to go and see the boss directly to sort out a problem." This creates some kind of vicious circle: "The instructions may be clear, but the fact that there are exceptions in certain cases means that everyone wants to take advantage of these exceptions."

How to gain recognition?

The question of recognition seems especially crucial. Employees seem willing to view difficult conditions in an acceptable light: "I'm this company's child and this factory's child, I can put up with the conditions in this factory." But they have a keen desire for everyone to be recognized equally.

The idea of differentiated treatment conjures up very strong images:

> Now, among the employees, there is a feeling of injustice, sometimes even of oppression. Those people have been hired, their salaries are higher than ours, and they get more special favors than us. This is why they detest Lafarge and they feel frightened . . . For example, for senior management, when they began to bring in employees from abroad . . . that led to a feeling of fear for most company employees, whether they were technicians or engineers . . . They envy each other.

The way that employees would like the company to operate (constantly reiterated in statements such as "there should be . . .") is closely tied to their wish to avoid the intensely frustrating feeling that some receive more recognition than others. This applies to both line and peer relationships.

While a great deal is expected from a leader who gives direction, he must also be seen as belonging to the same world as those he leads. On this count, it is essential to have a "reference" that is "the same" for all, for "me, as a simple employee, and you as top manager." The same holds true regarding the manager's presence among his subordinates: both a physical presence (sharing "breakfast or a cup of tea with him") and a moral presence, to the point of "being with him body and soul." The image of a paternal relationship, which we will return to later, was used to describe the expected relational style, blending authority and closeness. This implicitly reflects the opposition between the fundamental equality of such relationships (we belong to the same family, we hold the same place in society) and the radical inequality between master and slave.[3]

The fear that peers will be treated differently is also strong: "It [the company] must recognize each person's work. If my father preferred my brother to me, nothing would bind us together." In these circumstances, "the people here prefer a communist way of managing salaries." But, the speaker adds, "at the same time they want individuals to be recognized." Everyone wants to be recognized personally as equal to others and not simply as a nondescript part of an undifferentiated group: "Projects presented by people, and which prove useful for work, must have a specific advantage for those who propose them. Me, I want my proposal to have a financial reward."

Ideally, of course, recognition of each person's contribution (equity) would dovetail with the same treatment for all (equality); "our objective must be equity and equality [*al-adalaa wa al-moussaout*]". But how is this to be put into practice if people do not have equal capabilities?

Accommodating foreign management

The management changes that Lafarge is seeking to promote have given rise to very mixed reactions. There is a rejection of everything that gives the impression of a perpetually divided world where some are excluded from full membership of a community that gives preference to no one. On the contrary, anything that seems conducive to the advent of a form of unity promoting equal recognition for all raises high hopes.

The difficulty of openly challenging people

The *Principles of Action* were adapted locally into Arabic, without consultation with the parent company, by a committee of Jordanian managers working from the American version. Various passages were either not included or in all events radically changed. The passages in question involve eventual causes of humiliation, whether it be negatively evaluating an individual's action or criticizing their point of view.

Everything in the English version of *Principles of Action* related to personal shortcomings, failure, mistakes, weakness, and imperfections ("address repeated failure," "to learn from their . . . mistakes," "to compensate for our weakness and shortcomings") was omitted from the Arabic version. Thus, for example, the passage "They [the managers] . . . help them [employees] to learn from their achievements and mistakes" is rendered in the Arabic version by: "Regularly provide employees with constructive observations on their output."

In parallel, major changes were made to all references to individual performance appraisal. Thus, the passage: "Managers are expected . . . to evaluate results fairly and consistently" was omitted, as was: "we want all of our people to be able to measure and understand the impact and consequences of their actions."

In the section on teamwork, the passages referring to conflict ("dealing with conflict is an integral part of teamwork") and even differences of opinion or lack of consensus ("Teamwork is not about reaching consensus on every issue. It is about each individual . . . seeking differences of opinion as a source of progress") were quite simply dropped in the Arabic version.

The same fate befell the passages that mention situations involving tensions, such as "being a 'multi-local' organization involves . . . Involving Business Unit management teams in addressing the permanent conflicts that arise from operating globally in local businesses" and "managing the tension between 'local' and 'global' is one of the key challenges of our Group."

At the same time, efforts consistent with the managerial logic of clarifying each individual's responsibilities and evaluating their performance so as to treat them appropriately are struggling to succeed. This has drawn complaints from different expatriates.

According to the chief executive: "We have head office which has taken a bit of distance from the factories saying: 'You have your responsibilities, you have your objectives, we will leave you to get on with the job, but of course you remain accountable'." However, in practice, "when the news is good, as a rule people take it well, and when not always very pleasant feedback has to be given in appraisal interviews, when unpleasant, objective but not always positive, feedback has to be given, people don't do it." Likewise, for a French expatriate:

> there is a problem with delegation: I delegate a task to someone, who in turn delegates it to someone else . . . Afterwards, when I ask the person for feedback, they tell me "It's not me who performed the task" and ask me to see the person who did . . . In this case, only the task is delegated and the responsibility remains centralized, and in the end the decision comes back to me.

Or again, for another expatriate from a neighboring country: "Culturally, in this country, if you don't give someone a positive appraisal, this means that you don't want them to get a good pay rise, which means that you are against them." In parallel, initiatives likely to attract criticism tend to be avoided:

> If I don't work, nobody will notice any mistakes, which means that I am good, so I'll get promoted. This philosophy is very common unfortunately. Many people say: "If I have a high objective and I don't reach it, in the end I'll be seen as negligent." No, I set myself an objective that I am sure to reach.

The performance culture that the Group wants to develop is struggling to take shape (on this count, it is the opposite of what is happening in the Chinese subsidiary). When results are lacking, emphasis is laid on good intentions. "In case of a mistake, the Jordanian employee will say: 'I didn't do it on purpose, my intentions were good, so why are you assessing me on something I didn't mean to do?'"[4] Certainly, the emphasis on intentions does not only apply to situations where results are problematic; when the term "performance" is translated into Arabic in the local *Principles of Action*, the word used, *adda*, refers more to the way of acting than actual results. But this understanding of things can also serve as a form of self-protection.

There is also an impact on group work:

> People help each other. But nonetheless each person has their specificities and doesn't want anyone to intervene in their work . . . If you intervene in their work, it means that you will find mistakes, so, no, I close up and don't give anything . . . This attitude exists. And really, it does hinder group work.

Attempts at reform meant to challenge a very egalitarian pay system have been unfavorably received. Here again, the expatriates complain:

> I set a bonus for the high-performing executives; the news got around and the following day, certain people came to see me to explain that the individual bonuses had to be shared out among everyone to avoid problems . . . The second time, I opted for a secret appraisal process and decided to delay revealing the names until the last minute so as to avoid that kind of incident . . . When giving the thank-you letters and the bonuses, I realized that the secretary already knew the names of the people concerned, it was an open secret and I realized it was the cashier who had spread the news!

These reactions are more understandable if one keeps in mind the vision of the society that fuels them. Depending on the way they are treated, each individual feels somewhat like a son who enjoys all the indulgent affection of a father and the dignity that goes with this status or, on the contrary, like a servant (or even a slave) who is treated unsparingly and constantly made to feel humiliated by their inferior position. Anything that conflicts with the treatment a son would receive causes an individual to feel that he is being tipped into the status of a servant (slave). "Unpleasant feedback" is to be interpreted in the light of this opposition. There is thus a strong desire for a form of symbolic equality to be maintained, despite the disparities in skills and performance. And we can suppose that a keen awareness of just how fragile this equality is leads to a mistrust of anything that could damage it—even a somewhat lively discussion, in which a clash of ideas could quickly degenerate into *ad hominem* attacks laden with humiliating remarks.

Consult and advise

Although there are strong reserves against all forms of relationship likely to make some people feel inferior in status, a favorable reception is given to alternative paths that pave the way for non-confrontational exchanges of views in which people feel fully recognized. Listening and information sharing are thus highly valued.

The ideal leader is seen as someone who involves those under his responsibility in his projects by informing and consulting them:

> Frankly, the first thing, it's when you explain to an employee the company's vision, what its objectives are, then he feels on the side of general management, that he's progressing with it . . . You have to involve the people around you, so that they help you . . . When you involve him in decision-making, and you tell him: "we want to do this, what do you think about it?," then he becomes a stakeholder in your project.
>
> For the employee to participate, I have to inform him . . . I have to consult him, and then I involve him in the decision-making and by doing so he becomes responsible. Me, I compare him to a child at home, responsibility and the sense of belonging to a family is present from an early age, it's hereditary. But if the parent takes no notice of him, with time, it's sure that the responsibility and the sense of belonging will wane.

Criticism, which places the person on the receiving end in an inferior position, is ill accepted: "Criticism, me, I don't criticize directly . . . When I arrived, I had a clash with the people here. It was only a joke, but it degenerated, and turned into a dispute and problems." But this is not the case for advice, which on the contrary carries no risk of humiliation (Box 3.3). "We aren't used to criticizing openly. The way criticism is given is very important. It needs to be expressed as a recommendation [*nasihaa*] that you give to someone you wish well"; "Constructive criticism is a piece of advice that is not intended to harm the employee." When you have no desire to "harm" and even "wish well," you do not go beyond mentioning ways for improvement, and remain silent about what underlies the need for self-improvement. It is insulting to tell people that they have acted badly, but not if you suggest to them better ways of reaching their goals.

At the same time, a preference for a form of collective responsibility can be heard: "I find that working in a team is more relaxing because the responsibility is shared by everyone." "We like teamwork because teamwork is more comfortable for us. Because the responsibility is assumed by everyone. If I work on repairing a tool, and I work with one or two colleagues, then it's the responsibility of more than one person." Should things go wrong, no one has to carry the burden of failure individually, with the implicit prospect of being relegated to a lower status. There is thus no need for prudent strategies to avert the risk of

---

Box 3.3   Criticism and advice

As for constructive criticism, it's not that it isn't true but it isn't precise. That's not the exact way of putting it. Constructive criticism doesn't vex anyone. Here, subordinates never stop criticizing their bosses: that it would be good to improve this point, etc. but it's the way the criticism is made. And originally criticism in our culture is advice. And criticism can be considered as advice . . . Sometimes someone criticizes you in front of others and you take it as an insult, not advice.

My idea of constructive criticism is that I do a specific job, and my colleague says to me: "no, you can take a faster way to do this job, this job that you finished in half an hour, I can show you a way of tackling it and the job will take you five minutes." That's constructive criticism, that the job instead of taking half an hour will take you five minutes. That's a criticism that helps you to improve your work.

The manager has to emphasize the brighter points of an employee's life or an employee's work. If he is good and hard-working, he has to thank him and praise him, and give him the roll of honor and a bonus . . . Afterwards, the employee even accepts constructive criticism. Me, for example, I'm asked for five objectives or five duties, and I only do two, even so, I accept constructive criticism from my boss, because it's for my own good, he tells me: "you must find your motivation and work to develop yourself."

being badly judged: "The first thing, is that they see themselves as a group, which pushes employees to work with dedication, and stop calculating what work they do."[5]

L.F.T. and recognition for all

While anything likely to reduce an individual to a lower status meets with resistance, the prospect of finally overcoming the divisions between the upper and lower tiers of the company has been welcomed. The L.F.T. program has raised high hopes in this respect.

In the Arabic version of the *Principles of Action*, there is the added mention of "the mutual recognition of each person's contribution to the collective work," which is absent in the American version. When focus is placed on the fact that each person has contributed to the common venture to the best of their ability, rather than on weighing up each individual contribution, everyone can feel fully recognized.

Everyone, it is hoped, will be treated as full members of the community, whatever their position within the company: "The L.F.T. program . . . is doubtless a good program . . . It sets out a clear vision for the employees, and it involves everyone. It gives them prospects, encourages them, and gives them the feeling that their opinion counts."

> They talked about programs and that there would be training, etc. We hope so, so that we can progress in line with this development, so that we'll have a role, so that we'll have a share. So that these courses and training will not be restricted to a specific category. We're talking about the whole company, all the employees, not a specific category . . . When you give privileges to directors and department heads, and also privileges to the rest of the employees, and training courses, and you make them feel that the company pays attention to them, then they'll perform better, be more productive and more keenly interested.

By forming "a single team," the divide between management and the rank and file can be transcended:

> If all these executives, all these positions get together to make a decision, it's sure that the discussion will be constructive, because the opinions from the rank and file through to management level have been gathered to make the decision . . . And I hope that J.C.F., within the Lafarge Group, aims to reach that step. That we work as a single team, a single department.

The emergence of management through example is much awaited:

> Leadership through example is 100 percent important. For me, leadership through example, it's like a son following his father or mother, it's exactly the same thing. How can you be an ideal mother or an ideal father if you don't have behave in an exemplary manner, how can you expect your son to follow you if you say things and don't put them into practice. *"Alkoudoua,"* being an example, it's like the Prophet when he set the example, he did everything correctly and afterwards people followed his example.

A form of leadership with a strong moral overtone should produce leaders who, while setting a firm direction, remain close to those under their authority, like the father with his son, thus doing away with the haughty distance that so many complain about.

The implementation of rules and procedures and the strict definition of responsibilities so as to limit arbitrary conduct will no doubt be key ingredients in bringing about an orderly world where no one feels threatened by having to face the master's whims. "If there are work procedures, if there are clear steps, if responsibilities are defined and if there is a job description, then responsibility will be clearer for any work carried out." "This means that we will leave the exceptions, complications and conflicts behind."

Looking ahead, there are prospects for creating a "unified"[6] vision: "L.F.T. is important because it clarifies the corporate vision. It enables us to have *unifying, homogeneous* [our emphasis] principles." "It creates a *unified* vision of our mission within the company: a *common*, standardized language, *shared* by everyone. We have a single common goal and we know where we're going."

> The main idea I have of the L.F.T. project is that there has been a *unification* of objectives concerning the factory employees or company employees. This means that the company employees have *a single objective, a single vision* in their career at J.C.F. This is the most important idea that I have retained from this meeting [to present the project]. In addition to changing the work culture for company employees, that's to say, creating *a single culture*.

The very first achievements gave employees the feeling that a real step had been made in the direction of genuine change that had the potential to bring everyone closer together irrespective of their hierarchical position, including the chief executive, in a sort of symbolic equality transcending differences in rank:

The employees like the idea of L.F.T., especially since the L.F.T. day enabled employees working in different places and different divisions to get together around the same table and listen to the chief executive explaining the company's situation, its challenges, its vision.

What I appreciated, for example, in the L.F.T. day is being able to have an open discussion with the chief executive, you could ask him any question and that's very interesting, any question that came to mind concerning the company, you could ask the chief executive and he will give you a frank and honest reply.

For once, there was an exchange between people belonging to different factories and holding different levels in the hierarchy: cross-functional work groups.

How far will the drive for change go?

This latest attempt at reform raises a good many questions: will it go no further than slogans or will life in the subsidiary genuinely change? The experience of past reforms leaves some room for doubt. Changes have certainly occurred but their impact is open to question:

We expect a European mentality that treats people with civility and which manages things through key objectives, but on the ground there's no sign of all that, there's a change but it's not up to our expectations, there's a change but there's still the problem of making relationships personal.

"It still depends on the relationship between the employee and his boss." The change has had a very uneven impact on the company:

Things have changed, there have been big changes. Speaking from the productivity angle, productivity has become very important, and this certainly brings benefits. That was the most important side. The other thing is on the level of human resources, there has also been a big change.

But differential treatment still exists, which means that some people remain on the periphery of a community where everyone recognizes the others as being equal: "We, the older employees, we haven't seen any change, I mean development. Most of the focus was on maintenance staff, engineers, directors, whereas for us department heads or administrative staff, there hasn't been much . . . ."

Although L.F.T. seems promising, many people were wondering at the time of our survey to what extent the avenues it opened up would actually be explored: "What we lack is effective implementation of all that. And we hope that it will start to be applied, *Inshallah*." Some people had serious doubts: "It's a great project and we're afraid that it won't become reality." "The intentions are good but there aren't any methods to put them into practice." Again, we find the "must" register:

> If we don't have any work plans, and a schedule, people will say that it's just lip service . . . My employee *must* know what I do in L.F.T. I *must* get this message across: that I never stop working for you . . . So that he really feels there is something new on board and that he *must* participate in it.

Here again comes the assertion that everyone must be involved: "So if he [the employee] participates in this project, the project will succeed, and if he doesn't participate, the project won't succeed."

A cultural setting

The tensions and hopes that mark company life, and especially the expectations concerning the approach to change under the L.F.T. program, are linked to a vision of life in society that marks its cultural environment.

Like China, Jordan does not belong to the Western world, and this in itself explains why no great value is placed on the confrontation between different viewpoints and on uncompromising criticism of established views, both of which are important to the workings of a democratic society. In this respect, it is the West that is the odd one out. Yet, this certainly does not mean that elsewhere division is absent and a certain harmony reigns but rather that, in a large area of the world, situations of division or opposition need to be managed more diplomatically, failing which these could escalate into bloody conflict. What indeed is lacking are interpretative mechanisms allowing even lively discussions to be experienced in a way that is positive enough to avoid the risk of escalating violence.

Moreover, the admission of weakness and mistakes is likely to take on a positive meaning in Western societies, particularly in the United States, thanks to a variety of images that are doubtless not unrelated: the image of the sinner who repents, publicly as well in front of his brothers, and ends up stronger; that of the researcher stumbling in search of a hidden truth; or that of the man who, mindful of his own interest, learns from his failures. These images, which all share the notion of succeeding through failure or attaining greatness through abasement, are in no way universal in scope. Even in societies with a European culture, the place they hold is far from uniform. It is much more important in the United States, which is deeply marked by a vision of humanity based on a Christian heritage, than in France, where the admission of weakness is more readily seen as humiliating (d'Iribarne, 2002). Other cultures also give a positive sense to failure using other images. Thus, in China or Viet Nam, focusing on the lessons to be drawn from failure and on the fact that, in spite of everything, one has done one's best helps people to face up to failure. Considering what we observed, Jordanian society does not appear to have equivalent interpretative mechanisms, or at least these do not seem to be widespread.

The strong tension observed in the company between the celebrated ideal and day-to-day experience can be linked to the coexistence of two broad conceptions of what living together means in Jordanian society, which remains torn between the two.

As Ibn Khaldûn asserts in *The Muqqdimah* (1967 [1377–1402]), Arab societies are organized into tribes of differing degrees of nobility competing for power. In modern Jordanian society, and particularly in the corporate sector, the role of these "tribes" in the traditional sense is certainly not what it was in the past. Yet, this in no way means that what can still be described as a "tribal" logic has disappeared, in the sense that there is still an ensemble of groups, seen as more or less noble, within which solidarity is strong and which compete with one another. There is still a deep attachment to a form of honor that makes individuals highly sensitive to the way in which they are treated.[7]

This logic exists alongside a faith-based vision that celebrates a community inspired by a common ideal and governed by rules equally applicable to all. It is led by a guide, modeled on the Prophet, who acts justly and sets the example.

Ibn Khaldûn, when describing the world of his times (late fourteenth century), states that only an ideal such as this was able to create a degree of unity within the Arab world:

> Indeed . . . they [the Arabs] are of all peoples, too stubborn to accept the authority of others, on account of their coarseness, pride, ambition and jealousy. Their aspirations rarely tend towards a single goal. They need the influence of religious law, through prophecy or saintliness, to enable them to exercise self-restraint and divest themselves of their haughty and jealous character. It thus becomes easy for them to submit and unite, thanks to their religious

community . . . When a prophet or a saint, from among them, calls on them to observe God's commandments, rids them of their faults to replace these with virtues, requires them to unite all their voices so that truth triumphs, they then become fully united and achieve superiority and royal power.[8]

The same role played by a power with religious and moral legitimacy is also found in the political history of contemporary Jordan (Charillon and Kassay, 2002). From what we observed, this type of power can still be counted on to overcome "tribal" differences.

While providing a key reference for employees, a faith-based vision rarely informs company practices.[9] However, it could well materialize with the emergence of a moral community in which the distinction between levels of greater and lesser nobility loses its force. The existence of minutely defined and clearly established rules that apply to all, along with managers who willingly mix with their subordinates, involve them in their own preoccupations, consult them, respect their prerogatives, and more generally take an interest in their existence, evidences that there has been a change of worlds. Each individual, however modest their function, can thus feel that they are no longer prey to the contempt experienced by lower-ranking employees.

In this shift to a religious vision of society, there is little room for anything that signals division. From a religious viewpoint, as shaped by the Qur'an, division and even discussion are perceived very negatively. "Do not separate" (Pickthall, 1992, III:103). "And be ye not as those who separated and disputed after the clear proofs had come unto them" (III:105); "Say: Allah. Then leave them to their play of cavilling" (VI:91); "Lo! the devils do inspire their minions to dispute with you" (VI:121); etc. Conflicting views and divisions are a reminder of a tribal society in which clans oppose one another. The same holds true for criticism, which, in this type of society, is the privilege of those in the ruler's camp to be leveled against those they dominate, in which case a criticism constitutes a "personal offense."

By contrast, a great deal is expected from a form of leadership that leads to a shift away from tribal divisions, leaders' arbitrary conduct, and contempt for lowly folk towards a combination of moral rectitude and compliance with the rules. This does not mean establishing a certain power balance that is associated with lively debate and modeled on a Western vision of democracy, but rather (as in China, albeit in a very different mould) setting up a power that is benevolent and just, and at the same time firm.

Conclusion

What is expected from Lafarge in its Jordanian subsidiary is that the Group's action helps to put an end to the gulf separating those who lead and those who execute, to favoritism, and to the arbitrary exercise of power. The wish to have leaders who care about each individual, and who set an example of great moral rectitude, is very much present in Jordanian society. These leaders must ensure that there is a strict compliance with clearly defined rules applicable to all alike. Nurtured by a religious vision inspired by Islam, this wish goes hand in hand with an aspiration for a radical form of unity. Yet, these aspirations come up against a "tribal" notion of society that de facto exerts enormous influence on the ordinary corporate practices. The Group's proposed approach to implementing change was presented to the executive staff and offered the foretaste of a transformation that could well ensure full recognition for everyone, regardless of their job position. Hopes are high that this reference model of how to live together in harmony will eventually underpin the company's day-to-day life.

Notes

1   At the time of our investigations, the changes brought on by the privatization of this state-owned enterprise—characterized by close-knit ties with the local community, low productivity requirements, and a quagmire of routine—had not been fully digested. There were still strong local pressures in matters of hiring. Some of the employees supported the changes linked to the privatization, but others resisted them. As in our Chinese study, we do not deal with how this transition phase was managed.
2   Héla Yousfi also translated the interviews into French and helped to ensure the necessary interpreting (Yousfi, 2007).
3   For the role of this opposition in the Arab world, cf. Zghal (1994).
4   The Prophet's saying, "actions are judged by intentions," is often quoted; the result of an action is thus relegated to secondary importance.
5   Commenting on a first version of this text, the subsidiary's chief executive at the time this version was written (late 2008) underlined the practical importance of this point: "The initiatives for recognition failed as long as their purpose was to reward individuals; they became really successful when the purpose was to reward teams."
6   "Unified" is the literal translation from Arabic, but the Arabic word may also be translated by "homogeneous."
7   This form differs greatly from the French form as it does not make the same linkage between the register of honor and that of attachment to work done well out of a sense of professional duty.
8   Ibn Khaldûn, *op. cit.*, Vol. 1, Chapter 2, §26 "Arabs can obtain royal authority only by making use of some religious coloring, such as prophecy, or sainthood, or some great religious event in general."

9   This is not specific to Jordan. Thus, according to Clifford Geertz,

> In Morocco, the basis of ordinary life is secular enough to suit the most dedicated rationalist. And religious considerations for all their intensity are operative only over a few, very well demarcated regions of behaviour, so that one gets a ruthlessness in, for example, commercial and political affairs, which, at its most egregious, reminds one of the piquant combinations of professional brutality and personal piety one finds in some American racketeers.

> (Geertz, 1968: 112–113)

4 Local forms of support in all their diversity
A comparative survey

Following the launch of the L.F.T. program to diffuse knowledge of the Group's *Principles of Action* and gain support for the corporate values across all its subsidiaries, a questionnaire survey was conducted involving all employees. The survey, titled the *Employee Feedback Survey*, aimed to capture the reactions to this approach through questions on how each employee felt they were treated by the company (safety, recognition for work done, compensation, etc.), on the organization of their work, and on their engagement in the company.

The survey provided a substantial mass of data (several hundred thousand items) giving, for each of the questions asked, information on the differences between and within countries according to multiple criteria (site, professional activity, hierarchical level, gender, seniority).

Interpreting the scores (percentage of positive responses to questions asking the respondent whether they agree or disagree with a series of statements) for each question is rarely a straightforward matter. The responses are likely to be influenced by multiple factors and a respondent's objective experience is not the sole aspect that needs to be taken into account. What a question evokes within a specific social and cultural context also influences the response. So do the social norms that affect the way employees express their opinion when questioned by the company they work for. The survey, however, does not provide any elements on these points. Yet, for our approach, it is useful to compare each country's results. To begin with, this comparison has the advantage of showing to what extent a widespread and often unchallenged traditional view of the relationships between a company and its employees is linked to a particular cultural setting.[1]

We focused our attention on the survey data for two groups of countries: on the one hand, France and the United States, countries where the Group has most of its roots and that typify the Western world; and, on the other hand, China, Jordan, and Malaysia, countries where the

Group started up much more recently and for which our own qualitative survey helped to interpret data from the *Employee Feedback Survey*. After analyzing thousands of figures, we came up with a good many results on various aspects of the functioning of individual subsidiaries (which we do not report here), but also with several findings of a more general nature.

We see that some "obvious truths," underpinned by the experience of Western countries, about employee support for corporate policy cease to apply outside of these countries. The idea that senior management show the strongest support for their company, its values, and its policies concords with the results of the survey in the United States and France. However, it sits ill with what is observed in China, Malaysia, and Jordan. Similarly, we find no simple and universal relationship between the varyingly favorable judgments on the company and its policies (and therefore, one might think, the willingness to help implement these) and the sense of belonging to the company.

We then look at how employee attitudes towards the company differ substantially across work sites within one and the same country. This result confirms the findings of qualitative approaches showing that the influence of a culture in no way leads to stereotyped uniform attitudes. No cultural inevitability prevents management from seeking to foster those attitudes, out of a many possible ones, that are the most conducive to the efficient operation of a company.

To conclude, we examine the overall reactions to the initiative to launch the L.F.T. program with its goal of diffusing the company's values among the employees. We see how atypical the French are on this subject on account of their skepticism. Awareness of this peculiarity should prompt French personnel holding positions of responsibility in multinational corporations to pay much greater attention than they would automatically do to how this type of program is rolled out.

Employee support for the company and its policies: cultural logics

Company approaches to mobilizing employees are on the whole based on a vision, chiefly constructed around what is found in the old industrial countries, of what determines employee support for corporate policies. There is still little awareness of the cultural dimension of this support. Yet, the survey shows that this dimension is crucial. The influence of hierarchical level on an employee's overall attitude towards her or his company is particularly relevant. This also the case for the relationship between the employees' feeling of being well treated and their depth of engagement in the company.[2] On both counts, the United States and France indeed show responses in line with the usual view of company–employee relations: the more senior the job position, the more positive the attitude towards the company, and the better an employee feels treated, the greater their engagement. But the responses in Malaysia, China, and Jordan do not concord with this view. This finding gives good reason to be attentive to the wide variety of forms that the relationship between a company and its employees may take, and this variety is itself linked to the different understandings of what working for a company means.[3]

Hierarchical level and support for the company and its policies

In the most widespread view of how a company functions, the higher an employee's job position, the more they identify with the company and the stronger their support for its policies. Senior managers identify more with the company than lower managerial staff, and the latter more than the workfloor. The workfloor is often seen as readily confrontational, and it is this level that first springs to mind whenever the difficulties inherent to managing industrial relations are raised.

The survey data are consistent with this view for the United States and France. The questions involving the extent to which employees view their company favorably or their level of support for the company and its values almost systematically obtain more positive results the higher the respondent's rank in the hierarchy. Yet, much the opposite transpires in Malaysia, while in China and Jordan this correlation is far from systematic. This would suggest that, in the latter countries, the company's relationships with its employees are of a different nature than those posited in the traditional view.

We can gain a good idea of cross-country divergences by looking more closely at the responses to a few particularly telling questions and comparing the scores (i.e. the number of positive responses) of senior managers with those from the workfloor. The difference between these scores serves as a sort of measure of the difference in attitudes towards the company.

The United States and France have what may be termed a "classic" profile. Let us take, for instance, a statement that very directly expresses the overall relationship to the company: "I feel a strong sense of commitment to my company"/"*J'ai un fort sentiment d'appartenance à mon entreprise*" ("I have a strong sense of belonging to my company").[4] The scores for senior managers and the workfloor, and the differences between these scores, are reported in Table 4.1.

Table 4.1 Commitment scores

	North America[5]	France
Senior managers	90	97
Workfloor	60	74
Difference	+30	+23

In both the United States and France the score is significantly higher for senior managers than for the workfloor (+30 in the United States, +23 in France).

The same type of difference between senior managers and workfloor was also elicited by questions on statements reflecting views on the company:

- "Managers demonstrate through their actions that safety is their number one priority"/"*La direction et l'encadrement prouvent par leurs actes quotidiens que la sécurité est leur priorité numéro 1*" ("Executives and supervisors prove, through their day-to-day actions, that safety is their number one priority").
- "When I do a good job, my performance is rewarded"/"*Quand mon travail est bien fait, il est récompensé*" ("When my job is well done, I am rewarded").
- "Since we started Leader for Tomorrow in our company, I have seen some improvement in: the way I am managed"/"*Depuis le début du L.F.T., j'ai constaté une amélioration dans la façon dont je suis dirigé*" ("Since the start-up of L.F.T., I have noticed an improvement in the way I am managed").

On each question, the senior managers score higher than the workfloor, both in France (+19, +45, +14) and the United States (+29, +48, +18).

This is far from the case in Malaysia. For the four statements mentioned above, senior managers return a lower score than the workfloor, and sometimes markedly so (–3, –2, –3 and –17 respectively).

How can we make sense of these differences between senior managers and the workfloor, which are found in the responses to almost all of the questions?[6] Evidently, depending on the culture, each person's relationship with their company is not affected in the same way by the position they hold.

In France, the sense of belonging to a company is virtually taken for granted for senior managers, who are seen as in some way embodying the organization (see the French version of the *Principles of Action*). The same holds for the United States regarding senior managers' loyalty to their company. In both countries, this relationship is far more problematic for workfloor employees, as the rank and file has a staunch tradition of leveling criticism at the business world. Expressing a positive relationship with your company is much more admissible if you are in a position of power; the weight of the democratic model in fact makes it difficult to reconcile the status of an employed worker subject to the authority of a whole chain of command and the status of a free citizen equal to all others.

At the same time, the workfloor environment in the United States offers a greater variety of scenarios than in France. In France, asserting a distance from corporate goals (i.e. doing one's job more than serving the company) is very generally part and parcel of the workfloor culture. It is hardly honorable for someone in a subordinate position to be overly complacent towards the company they work for. Moreover, although the actual notion of "belonging" is acceptable to a low-level worker if "company" is taken to mean the community of one's fellow workers, this is not the case when identified with management and shareholders. In the United States, support from workfloor employees can be very robust in a company with a strong sense of community, but very weak in a company where a strict contractual logic is coupled with strained labor relations (we come back to this point regarding the differences in responses between plants in the same country).

In Malaysia, we do not find the same difficulty in reconciling the status of employed worker with that of a free citizen in a democratic society. Working under the authority of a superior does not raise problems of principle. There is no risk of being accused of "class collaboration" or of behaving like "Uncle Tom" for celebrating one's company. In a qualitative survey we conducted there,[7] we gathered statements such as:

> In people's mindset, especially for Malay and Indian, we have to follow whatever has been set up, has been ruled by the person that you respect. Even in the family or in the group or in the company. This is why people think whatever has been ordered by the top boss, they will think you have to follow . . . We have to follow and we have to commit to whatever has been instructed.

The word "commitment" implies a type of relationship with the company that is taken for granted. This does not mean employees demand less of those they report to, but their demands are not the same as in Western countries.

More broadly speaking, once outside the Western countries, hier-archical level does not appear to have a consistently favorable impact on the responses to the questions asked. In China and Jordan, senior managers reply more positively or less positively than the workfloor, depending on the question.[8]

Ultimately, the view that employees have a more favorable attitude toward their company when they are higher up the organization (or vice-versa, a less favorable attitude when they are lower down) is rooted in the way social relations typically function in Western societies. The fact that equality is a fundamental value in these societies means that it is difficult to find an acceptable meaning for situations involving subordination. Very different interpretations of such situations are to be found in other cultures.

Satisfaction and a sense of belonging

One might think that, regardless of culture, the personal satisfaction expressed by an employee in regard to company policies, and above all to the way they are treated, automatically correlates with a sense of belonging to the company. This type of correlation is clearly observed in countries such as France or the United States. This is confirmed by comparing the reactions of various hierarchical levels or, as we shall see, the reactions of different company sites with varyingly healthy social climates. It is likely to be the same case in other countries with European cultures. When we look further afield however, things seem less simple. The fact is that there is a great deal of culture-dependent diversity in the manner of belonging to a company. Moreover, using the word "belonging" to describe an employee's ties with a company without taking into account the relevant cultural setting is problematic. We have already seen that the word "*appartenance*" (belonging) used in the French version of the questionnaire is in no way synonymous with the word "commitment" in the English version. Using a familiar word (such as "belonging") to describe a type of relationship specific to a foreign culture that may be totally alien to our own experience is likely to be highly misleading. The fact that the same correlation is not found in the responses to some questions does not give us the key to understanding what is roughly equivalent elsewhere to the French interpretation of "belonging." But this at least prompts us to ask ourselves pertinent questions and to seek clarification using other approaches.

The feedback from the Jordanian employees clearly illustrates this phenomenon. Whereas Jordan scores the lowest out of the five countries examined for the statement "When I do a good job, my performance is rewarded," it returns the highest score for the question statement "I have a strong sense of commitment to my company." The contrast is particularly striking for senior managers. The percentage of positive responses for them is zero when it comes to how their work is rewarded and 100 percent when it comes to their sense of commitment. When an employee expresses their company loyalty, this is not linked to their reaction to the way they are treated. Emphasizing support for one's company, even though one claims to be badly treated, is highly regarded as this is seen as a form of moral loyalty. This is far removed from the humiliating implications it would have in France or the United States, where such support would be interpreted from a social and political viewpoint as submissive and alienating. In a culture governed by a so-called "tribal" logic, the sense of belonging is pivotal and quite distinct from the judgment an individual may make about their daily experience. When an individual fails to make known their membership of a group or their pride in belonging, even if they consider in-group behavior and events to be dramatic, this is seen as betrayal and self-depreciation.[9]

The same phenomenon is seen to a lesser extent in France, more particularly with workfloor employees, who score 74 percent of positive responses to the statement "I have a strong sense of belonging to my company," whereas the score is only 26 percent for the statement "When I do a good job, my performance is rewarded." This strong sense of commitment to their company, doubtless identified more as the community of their fellow workers rather than the shareholders and management, does not preclude them from adopting a critical attitude towards the latter.

In China the opposite is true. This is the country that returned the lowest scores for the statement on "commitment" and, at the same time, one of the highest scores for the statement "When I do a good job, my performance is rewarded."[10] As shown in our survey, Lafarge diverges from the traditional Chinese business model based on interpersonal networks with special relationships (*guanxi*). In the absence of strong ties, the employees choose to enter into an instrumental relationship with the company focused on opportunities for personal development within the company. These opportunities are much appreciated by the employees in Lafarge but does not instill a sense of "commitment." Furthermore, at the time of the survey, the employees were unsure as to the Group's future in China and its firm commitment in the country, which tended to encourage rather short-term, self-interested relationships with the company. This situation may have had an impact on the responses to the question on the sense of commitment.

This aspect should be taken into account in order to understand the sometimes surprising reactions of employees in the Chinese subsidiaries of international groups. Managers who are apparently quite satisfied with the company they work for (to describe it as "their" company would doubtless imply a relationship that does not reflect reality) frequently quit their job without the slightest warning. Such behavior surprises French managers, who tend to see belonging to a company as a form of allegiance implying a certain loyalty, and this relationship is expected to last unless relations become difficult and lead to a rupture. An unexpected resignation is especially shocking when, in the French mindset, it is felt that someone has "sold" themselves to earn a few dollars more. From a Chinese perspective, there is nothing surprising or shocking about this.

Chinese satisfaction without support and Jordanian support without satisfaction furnish an insight into forms of engagement other than the mix of market relations and community-based integration seen in the United States and the type of noble allegiance found in France.

The diversity revealed in the survey needs to be taken into full account when designing human resources policy. It should not be assumed that support from senior executives is so universally self-evident that it does not warrant concern, or even that creating a satisfying work environment will always be enough to ensure employee loyalty.

Culture, social climate, and relations with the company

Even within the same country, there can be very different responses to the same question depending on the particular work site. This in no way leads to the conclusion that cultural characteristics have no bearing on the responses, as could be thought if one imagines in line with an all too common image that a culture automatically leads to uniform social relations and hence to stereotyped responses to a question. What culture does influence is the actual type of within-country variations in the sphere of social relations as in other areas. Correspondingly, the existence of a shared culture does not bar management from favoring one or other of the very diverse forms of functioning that coexist within the same country. What is observed in France and the United States is once again especially significant, no doubt owing to the fact that establishing cooperative social relations in both these countries requires a particularly delicate alchemy.

The French disconnect between the relationship with one's company and the relationship with one's work

In France, the magnitude of the differences between the work sites that returned generally positive responses and those with generally negative ones varies greatly depending on the type of question. This comes clearly to light when we compare the scores of two factories—one of which (Saint-Paul-le-Château[11]) obtained particularly positive responses and the other (Bray) distinctly less so—and carefully investigate the differences between these scores.

The most notable divergences involve those questions that touch on how the actions of the company and its management, and the overall quality of company operations, are judged. This is true of questions on statements such as: *"La direction et l'encadrement prouvent par leurs actes quotidiens que la sécurité est leur priorité numéro 1"* ("Executives and supervisors prove, through their day-to-day actions, that safety is their number one priority") (+41 for Saint-Paul); *"Je dispose des moyens nécessaires pour fournir des produits et des services de qualité à nos clients externes"* ("I have the means required to provide quality products and services to our external customers") (+36; or *"En ce qui concerne le Lafarge Way, je pense que le comportement de la direction est respectueux des valeurs de l'entreprise"* ("Regarding the Lafarge Way, I think that the behavior of the management is respectful of the company values") (+22).

By contrast, the questions focusing on the respondents and their way of working do not show the same divergence. Thus, for the two statements in this register that begin with *"Je comprends"* ("I under-stand")—*"De quelle façon mon travail peut contribuer aux objectifs de l'entreprise"* and *"Les conséquences de mon travail sur la qualité des produits et services que nous fournissons à nos clients externes"* ("How my work can contribute to the company's objectives" and "The consequences of my work on the quality of products and services that we provide to our external customers")—the responses are virtually identical (with statistically insignificant differences).

The situation is midway for the statements relating to support for the company: *"J'ai un fort sentiment d'appartenance à mon entreprise"* ("I have a strong sense of belonging to my company") (+15); *"Je suis fier de travailler pour mon entreprise"* ("I am proud to work for my company") (+10), with a particularly high level of positive responses (89 and 79) to the latter question in both factories.

Finally, for the statement *"Lorsque mon travail est bien fait il est récompensé"* ("When my job is well done, I am rewarded"), the level of positive responses is almost identical, being very low in both factories (32 and 30).

In France, the manner of belonging to a company evidences a weak linkage between three clearly distinguishable types of employee rela-tionships: with company management, with the employee's own work, and with the company as a whole. Just because an employee's view of management is not very positive does not mean they will be any less committed to their work. Likewise, neither does it prevent them from taking pride in a sense of belonging to their company, which they identify with their fellow employees and not those running the company. Moreover, even when they enjoy excellent relations with their company, a certain unease is attached to the idea that they only take their work seriously if they are "rewarded," which would be considered dishonorable (the use of the word "*récompensé*" in the French questionnaire doubtless reflects an ill-fitting, albeit linguistically correct, translation of the American term "rewarded").

Is this to say that the commitment to one's job and the desire to do it well are such that the climate in the factory has no influence on how the company functions? This of course would be an overstatement. Even though the survey data do not inform us about the actual operation of each factory, we can see that cooperation between different workgroups is viewed as being substantially more positive in Saint-Paul (63) than in Bray (49)—and, in a French setting, this points to a particularly sensitive issue for the efficient running of operations (Segal, 2009).

The United States between strictly interest-based relations and community-based enterprise

In the United States even more than in France, significant differences are found between the responses from the various work sites. Moreover, we do not find the same type of diversity given that the forms of good and bad cooperation are not the same in the two countries. It is not the proud assertion of autonomy linked to a perfect command of one's *métier* that is key, but rather the combination of fairness in contractual relations and life in a community united around shared values. Relations can range from those showing strong support for the company and its goals—for example, the "excellent companies" such as I.B.M. and others operating on a community-based logic, praised by Peters and Waterman (1982)— to adversarial relations such as the ones the American automobile industry is finding it hard to avoid. While a sense of engagement in the company's success is the norm in the former, in the latter, we find a somewhat interest-based relationship.

To gain an insight into eventual divergences and their underlying logic, we can compare two sites that returned sharply contrasted responses: on the one hand, Bowling Green, with a very positive tenor and, on the other, Woodson, with a distinctly negative tenor. We once again focus on the differences between the scores at these two sites that came to light in responses to several statements.

There are substantial differences to the questions on statements relating to the way management acts: "Managers demonstrate through their actions that safety is their number one priority" (+46); "Regarding the Lafarge Way, I believe: management behavior is consistent with the values" (+ 59); and "I have the means in my job to provide quality products and services to our external customers" (+60).

Whereas in France the responses to questions concerning an individual's understanding of their work have little connection with the judgments made about the company and its leaders, the same is not true in the United States. The differences between Bowling Green and Woodson are very marked for the statements: "I have a clear understanding of how my work contributes to achieving my company's overall goals" (+32) and "I understand the impact of my job on the quality of products and services we supply to our external customers" (+34) (these questions returned the same scores at Saint-Paul and Bray). For the questions on statements related to a sense of engagement with the company, whereas the responses in France showed only slight differences, in the United States there were significant divergences: "I am proud to work for my company" (+34); "I feel a strong sense of commitment to my company" (+41). And for the question: "There is a good cooperation between my workgroup and other workgroups," the difference between sites (+53) is even greater than in France.

Contrary to what we observed in France, the response to the statement: "When I do a good job, my performance is rewarded" (+51) is closely tied to judgments about the company and its leaders. Whereas in France the employees are reluctant to say they are well "rewarded" even when they have excellent relations with the company (it is worth remembering that in the plant with the most positive responses overall, only 32 percent of employees answered "yes" when asked if this statement applied to them), in the United States the situation is strikingly different. At Bowling Green, 74 percent replied "yes."

The differences are narrower for questions on statements relating to the implementation of a system of objectives and performance measures: "I have clearly defined performance goals and objectives." For this statement, the gap is no more than ten points, with a high level of positive responses (72 percent) even where the overall tenor of responses is the worst.

The survey responses evidence a variant of a highly cooperative mode of functioning at the Salt Fleet factory. Here, scores are even higher than at Bowling Green for the questions relating to a sense of community.[12] They are not as high, however, for questions on evaluation and remuneration for individual performance.[13]

Relations between management and employees can be very diverse. On one side, as at Woodson, relations show a very low level of trust, which nonetheless poses no obstacle to the implementation of a system of objectives and evaluations ensuring a minimum of fairness within a contractual relationship. Yet, on the other side, we also come across very positive relations, with two variants: as at Bowling Green, positive relations based on a strong contractual element and sharp emphasis on evaluation and reward for individual performance; and, as at Salt Fleet, a more community-based variant, in which a vigorous collective dimension, coupled with the celebration of shared values, has successfully pushed personal attachment to recognition and reward for individual performance into a position of secondary importance.[14]

Reactions to the L.F.T. program: a French singularity

Three questions in the survey asked for responses related directly to the respondents' reactions to the L.F.T. program to diffuse group values among the subsidiaries:

* "Since we started Leader for Tomorrow in our Company, I have seen some improvements in: the way I do my job"/"*Depuis le début du projet L.F.T., j'ai constaté une amélioration dans: la façon dont je fais mon travail.*"
* "Since we started Leader for Tomorrow in our Company, I have seen some improvement in: the way I am managed"/"*Depuis le début du projet L.F.T., j'ai constaté une amélioration dans: la façon dont je suis dirigé.*"
* "Since we started Leader for Tomorrow in our Company, I have seen some improvements in: the way I work with others"/"*Depuis le début du projet L.F.T., j'ai constaté une amélioration dans: la façon dont je travaille avec les autres.*"

The first statment ("I have seen some improvements in: the way I do my job") gives the greatest variety of responses across countries. For the five countries studied, we separate out the average responses for all occupational categories combined, for senior managers, and for the workfloor, the percentages of positive responses being shown in Table 4.2.

Table 4.2 Job improvement scores

	North Am.	*France*	*China*	*Jordan*	*Malaysia*
Overall	30	16	71	49	76
Senior managers	38	24	69	27	60
Workfloor	24	15	73	62	84

Overall, the level of positive responses is very low for France (16 percent), high in Malaysia (76 percent) and China (71 percent), and moderate in the United States (30 percent) and Jordan (49 percent).[15]

The scores in France are particularly striking. Here, the score is very low for all occupational categories, from the workfloor (15) through to senior managers (24). In a breakdown by site, scores descend even further: 14 for the Bray factory and as low as 3 for Val d'Uzès. Even in a factory like Saint-Paul-le-Château, where responses are particularly positive overall, the score is no higher than 20. This result is all the more striking given that the question in itself does not imply an in-depth change in practices (referring simply to the fact of there having been some change, irrespective of how much).

One might have expected the responses in the United States to be the least positive. Certainly, it is not easy for Americans to concede that a program from French headquarters is able to transform the way they work. At Lafarge, American employees have long shown "a strongly particularist dimension and a relatively limited sense of belonging a group" (Collomb, 2007: 10). Yet even on this point, the scores are significantly higher than in France. In addition, at sites where the overall tenor of responses suggests a particularly good social climate, positive responses are in the majority (50 at Salt Fleet, 65 at Bowling Green), which is never the case in France.

The French skepticism towards the L.F.T. program is not driven by a lack of confidence in company leadership. The number of employees responding positively to the statement "*En ce qui concerne le Lafarge Way, je pense que le comportement de la direction est respectueux des valeurs de l'entreprise*" ("Regarding Lafarge Way, I think that: the behavior of the management is respectful of the company values") is much higher than those who state that their behavior has changed due to the implementation of L.F.T.[16] (although if we take the cross-country average, we find the same score for both questions). In the opinion of most of the French employees surveyed, the fact that the L.F.T. program has made little impact does not stem from management's failure to set the example; it is rather because the example set by management is not what drives the actions of individuals. Whatever relationship employees have with their company, they are keen to emphasize that they do their work on their own initiative, regardless of what the company tries to impose.[17] Moreover, in France it is not done to talk too much about corporate values, a fact that may also influence reactions to management approaches that foreground such values (d'Iribarne, 2002).[18]

This French reticence may lead employees, when asked, to understate the changes that actually occurred, whereas in other countries the opposite is true. Even those who changed their work methods due to the L.F.T. program will tend not to broadcast it. Additionally, the reluctance shown by employees at all echelons to allow themselves to be influenced by an L.F.T.-type program means that any change driven by this type of approach will indeed be modest.

The situation is quite different in the United States. It is not the proud assertion of autonomy linked to the perfect command of one's *métier* that dominates. When relations with the company are good, employees are less reluctant than their French counterparts to say that they have changed work methods, or indeed to progress because of their company's influence. Interestingly, in an English-language executive summary of another survey on the L.F.T. approach, the authors (consultants) had no qualms about differentiating between the "true believer," those with "limited faith," and "skeptics" to describe respondents' attitudes to the approach. Using religious vocabulary to talk about a company policy is natural in the United States, whereas this would be almost unthinkable in France, unless one is happy to make do with a literal translation from the American.

What is more, reactions in many countries to this type of approach run counter to those in France. This shows up clearly when we examine the responses to the survey questions concerning L.F.T. Considering overall results for each country, the level of positive responses to the statement about actual improvements in "the way I do my job" is 71 percent in China, 76 percent in Malaysia, and 49 percent in Jordan. In China, as comments from our qualitative survey show, the L.F.T. program dovetails perfectly with the leader's role of giving direction from the top, which encourages employees to take the approach very seriously. In Malaysia, we are in a society where the expectation, especially among the rank and file, is that direction comes from the top. In Jordan, senior managers have a far from positive score (27 percent) for this question and many others; their reactions should perhaps be interpreted as evidencing that they keep a proud distance from a foreign group. The same, though, is not true for workfloor employees, who also expect a great deal from their leaders.

Conclusion

One of the foremost lessons gleaned from our analysis of the *Employee Feedback Survey* is that the standard view of company–employee relationships—fostered by the example of Western countries—is a far cry from what exists in much of the world. This standard view fits with the survey results for France and the United States (and would likely fit broadly with results obtained in Western societies). In these countries, having the dual status of a subordinate worker and a citizen equal to one's peers in a democratic society is problematic, especially for low-level employees who feel mistreated by their company. At country level, the problems this raises are likely to be solved to very varying degrees from one place to another, which thus produces very uneven forms of cooperative functioning. By contrast, in the Asian countries (China, Malaysia, and Jordan) we do not find the same underlying problems with regard to subordination. In each of these countries, we see a specific form of company integration, and each form determines the sensitive points—which differ across cultures—that shape the level of employees' engagement and their contribution to the company's success.

In China, the relationship with the company is more interest-based. What matters above all are the opportunities for personal development, and an employee's loyalty to the company cannot be counted on if better opportunities are offered elsewhere. In Jordan, by contrast, we see a strong sense of belonging together with a heightened sensitivity to how one feels treated, which may well lead to very negative reactions towards the company. In Malaysia, especially among the rank and file, expectations are high with regard to guidance from above and leadership issues are particularly crucial.

The survey also confirms that we need to be wary of cultural representations that seek to characterize a culture simply on the basis of a few figures, as so often happens in academic studies on the role of culture in corporate management—and these are frequently used by companies to train executives in intercultural cooperation.[19] The extreme diversity of responses within one country, as is found in the United States and France, shows us that sharing the same culture in no way leads to uniform attitudes and behavior. Culture influences the type of diversity we find in a given country and particularly the diversity of company–employee relationships. It determines the form of both cooperative and uncooperative relations. However, a culture does not lead to any inevitable outcome regarding the varyingly cooperative level of relationships that develop between a company and its employees. From a management perspective, it is crucial to take this diversity into account when seeking to foster attitudes and behaviors conducive to the successful functioning of company—which is something we tend to forget if we buy into a representation of culture that has us believe attitudes and behaviors in each country are homogeneous.

Moreover, what characterizes a culture is the specific way in which employees integrate a company, and each has its own logic or coherence. In a questionnaire survey such as Lafarge's *Employee Feedback Survey*, this logic becomes apparent in the distinct patterns of coherence in the responses. It is vital to take this logic into account if we are to learn from such approaches. If we dismiss it, we are in danger of either too hastily using "bad" scores to point a finger at the entities that returned them or too hastily celebrating "good" scores, with the result that we overlook what the scores can really teach us. The fact remains that it is difficult to go from identifying a particular pattern of responses within a country to interpreting this pattern when we lack the data needed to understand what the questions mean in the respondents' mental universe. For this reason, any interpretation of this type of questionnaire survey needs to be grounded on research paths that open up access to the mental universe of the respondents.

Finally, a major lesson for the French. Their skepticism towards any approach involving the dissemination of corporate values is rooted in a very specifically French vision of work. They need be wary of thinking that in this respect the world is made in their image.

Notes

1 Moreover, a comparison of the responses from Lafarge and those collected by the same survey firm for other companies in equivalent environments generally showed Lafarge in a very favorable light. For example, Lafarge Ciments France scored twenty points higher than the average scores obtained in France for responses to the questions that seemed to best reveal the overall employee attitude to the company, such as "*Je suis fier de travailler pour mon entreprise*" ("I am proud to work for my company") or "*J'ai un fort sentiment d'appartenance à mon entreprise*" ("I have a strong sense of belonging to my company").

2 Other points emerged more or less clearly in the survey responses. This was notably the case for the general style of relations with the company. Thus, Malaysia stands out for the particularly positive tenor of responses overall. This is not to say that there are a majority of very high scores, but rather that no score is really low. Moreover, there are a significant number of neutral responses even for those questions with the highest rate of positive responses. Relations with the company are characterized by a strong concern for conformity coupled with a certain degree of neutrality, which reflects the local cultural norms. This is a far cry from the much more emotionally laden relationships, both positive and negative, found in Jordan.

3 Of course, data from this type of questionnaire survey do not *per se* provide insight into the specific type of coherence that characterizes the responses for each country. However, a deeper understanding becomes possible once sufficient knowledge has been acquired about the cultures that shape the respondents' mental universe. In this respect, the questionnaire survey and the qualitative approach enabling us to access this mental universe complement each other very well.

4 There is an appreciable difference in meaning between the French and English versions of the question; "commitment" is far from synonymous with "belonging." This is what we found regarding the French and English versions of the *Principles of Action* (a similar systematic comparison could be made between the two versions of the questionnaire). When interpreting the responses it is important to take into account exactly what the word evokes in the culture where the respondent is located.

5 The overall results for the United States were consolidated with those of the Canadian subsidiary into a "North American" group. Given the preponderance of the United States in this group, it seemed possible to liken the overall results with the form of social relations in the United States.

6 In France, out of the thirty-eight questions asked, only one obtained a score from senior managers that was lower, albeit with statistically insignificant difference, than the French average. And only three returned a score from workfloor employees that was higher, but again with a statistically insignificant difference, than the French average.

7 Survey conducted by Jean-Pierre Segal.

8 In China, they respond more positively to questions involving their "sense of commitment" (+11) and on how they are rewarded when they do their job well (+24), but less positively for the question on how L.F.T. affects the way they are managed (−22), with no difference for the question on safety. In Jordan, they are more positive for the first two questions (+9, +18), but less so for the last two (−15, −32).

9 This result is comparable with what we had observed with a qualitative survey in a Morocco-based company. Although the employees expressed a high level of satisfaction with everything work-related, as well as strong support for the company as a community where people live together, they were far less positive about their personal situation. There were even complaints that, from a French viewpoint, jarred with the rest of the interviews (d'Iribarne and Henry, 2007). In this survey Morocco's relative score (compared with other countries) for the question on the sense of belonging was distinctly better (though less spectacular than Jordan's) than for the question on the way in which employees are rewarded. This may well be a trait shared by the whole of the Arab world.

10 For senior managers, the score for the question about commitment is even lower (−8) than for the question on "work well rewarded."

11 We have used pseudonyms for the factories mentioned, both in France and the United States.

12 "Regarding the Lafarge Way, I believe: the values have been clearly communicated" (+21); "In my Company, we make a point of celebrating our successes" (+ 26).

13   "In my work group, we have indicators (KPI) to measure our performance regularly" (–22); "I understand how my performance is evaluated" (–6); and "When I do a good job, my performance is rewarded" (–24).

14   In China, unlike in France and the United States, there are only small (and statistically insignificant) differences between the survey responses from the various factories. The differences are more appreciable, though still small, in Malaysia and Jordan. We came up with no clear interpretation of these differences, perhaps because our knowledge of these societies is rather more limited than for France and the United States.

15   The French results for this question are very close to those for the questions on improvements in "the way I am managed" and "the way I work with others"; for the three questions the responses show similar divergences from the global average. France is unique in this respect for the three questions.

16   This contrast is found for France overall: 54 vs. 16. This is also the case for the various occupational categories: 82 vs. 24 for senior managers, 46 vs. 15 for workfloor employees. And the same is true across the different sites, 63 vs. 20 at Saint-Paul, 41 vs. 14 at Bray.

17   It is of note that, in France, the questions relating in some way to "*je connais mon travail*" ("I know my job") return relatively higher scores (compared with the cross-country average) than those relating to "*mes supérieurs me guident dans mon travail*" ("my superiors guide me in my work"). The importance of references to doing one's job on one's own initiative and drawing on one's own skills is reflected in a series of differences between responses on similar subjects approached from different angles. Thus, for the statement "*nous comprenons les besoins des clients externes*" ("we understand the needs of our external customers"), the score is higher (+4) than the average cross-country score, whereas the opposite is true for the statement "*je reçois des informations sur la satisfaction des clients externes*" ("I receive information about the satisfaction of external customers") (–5).

18   In the survey, this phenomenon is evidenced by the fact that the question on clear communication of values ("Regarding the Lafarge Way, I believe: the values provide clear direction for employees") has a mediocre score in France (40; –26 compared with the cross-country average).

19   The main reference in this field is Hofstede (1981, 2001).

5 Values materialize in harmony with individual cultures

We have observed several facets of the encounter between corporate values and a diversity of cultures. Yet, at the end of our journey, how can we gain insight into the way this encounter operates? To what extent have we found truly common values, which would suggest that they transcend cultural differences? And how does this common core of values take shape in each culture?

To answer these questions, we must first of all dispel a misunderstanding tied to the fact that a culture is most often identified with a set of values. We shall then return to the text in which Lafarge sets out its corporate vision and see that it closely interlinks three different registers: the invocation of universal values, the Group's choice to give priority to some of these values, and a manner of materializing these values that is specific to the Western world. Drawing a distinction between these registers will help us to identify how universal and cultural aspects have been intertwined in the company's approach. We shall then broaden our topic by taking a look first at life in multinational companies in general and then at how the universality-culture nexus operates on a wider scale.

Values and cultures

In its most widespread representation, culture is assimilated to a set of values that themselves shape practice. From this angle, it is difficult to understand how people can share the same values and yet, at the same time, behave differently within cultures that are themselves vastly different. The fact is that values and culture do not belong to the same sphere.[1]

When an individual or group talks about values, their reference is an ideal or a world that they would like to see materialize. They have no need to worry about the eventual real-world difficulties involved in combining the diverse values to which they are attached. In the abstract world of values, they can therefore call on tolerance and solidarity concurrently without having to ponder whether these are difficult to reconcile in real life; whether in relatively diversity-tolerant societies (India, United States), the solidarity between different communities living more or less peacefully together proves to be relatively weak; or whether societies with a relatively high level of solidarity (Scandinavian countries) typically have low tolerance towards diversity in their day-to-day functioning. We could compile a long list of paired values that can be advocated simultaneously as long as we remain in our ideal world, without the need to weigh up whether prioritizing one of them in the real world would mean sacrificing the other in some way: freedom and equality, the quest for excellence and respect for the weak, exaltation of the individual and of the community, mobility and the value of roots, etc. It is the privilege of Utopias to depict societies in which this kind of antinomy is overcome.

When we speak of cultures, we then slip back into down-to-earth constraints. We find holistic visions of societal life in which values are admittedly not absent, but the key concern then becomes finding a way to reconcile those that conflict, more or less, in practice. And this reconciliation involves a whole realm of compromise and half-measures, in which the reference values are not forgotten but where each of them is subject to various limitations so that they can materialize without jeopardizing the pursuit of other values. The absolute nature of values then gives way to the need for practical coherence. And each culture is characterized by the distinct way it makes a compromise between values that are hard to marry—a compromise that is itself colored by the distinct way of conceiving how these values translate into reality. Freedom is thus restricted in the name of equality and equality is restricted in the name of freedom. Taking an example from Germany, France, and the Anglo-Saxon world, we find in each setting a specific way of reconciling what is in fact a very relative form of freedom with an equally relative form of equality, with each approach having its own coherence (d'Iribarne, 2003, 2006).

In both the French and American versions, Lafarge's *Principles* simultaneously refer to the spheres of values and cultures. On one side, an ensemble of values is presented uncompromisingly, regardless of the eventual problems of reconciling them; while some values are especially foregrounded, emphasis is also laid on others that are difficult to integrate into a whole. On the other side, we find (with slight differences between the French and American versions) an outline of how these are to be implemented in the specific Franco-American cultural setting in which the *Principles* were defined. When we observe how management methods based on the Group's values have been received outside the countries in which they were developed, the difference between these two spheres is clear to see. On the one hand, some of the Group's values enjoy a positive, sometimes enthusiastic, reception. On the other hand, these values materialize in a form that differs from that found in the parent company.

Universal values

Lafarge's *Principles* give little place to an explicit statement of values. This only occurs in two short passages. The first: "Courage, integrity, commitment, consideration for others and an overriding concern for the Group's interests are the foundations of our management philosophy" and the second: "Respect for the common interest, openness and dialog, integrity and commitment are the main ethical principles of our Group and of our people." Yet, an implicit reference to values is omnipresent, be it those involving the attachment to unity and sharing or the affirmation of the individual.

The reference to a united community is central to the text. Putting a name to the related core value is not however a simple matter since any manner of doing so is culturally biased. But it can be suggested by a variety of terms that evoke its different facets: concern for others, sharing, solidarity, benevolence, unity, etc. By highlighting this value— which is far from the case of all companies—the Group is expressing a definite choice. It has undoubtedly been influenced in this by the fact that its corporate culture bears the imprint of the Christian humanism of its founders. This affects relations between employees, as well as the relations that the company maintains with its employees.

The term "sharing" recurs constantly. It is a matter of "creating an organization where our global experience and know-how are easily accessible to everyone and . . . *shared* [our emphasis]," "We expect our people to *share* their experiences," "Fostering an environment where information is widely available and openly *shared*." It is stated: "We expect our people to *share* their experiences and to seek those of others." "*Share* our local successes, regardless of their scale," "knowledge *sharing*," and "*share* our global experience" are mentioned. This sharing goes hand in hand with mutual support: "We want to promote an environment where individuals and teams . . . support, and are supported by the whole organization." Managers are expected to "help their people deal with potential performance issues" and employees are expected to be "willing to ask for help when they need it." Correspondingly, the aim is to offer "a uniquely participative and supportive environment . . . where daily interaction is founded on trust, respect, dialog and teamwork," to create "an environment of trust and confidence," and to build a "dialog between staff and line." The value of sharing, along with the associated support, confidence, and loyalty, is also mentioned, albeit more briefly, vis-à-vis relations with customers and shareholders. It is thus a moral duty to "share value creation with our customers and end-users." More generally, it is the company's responsibility to "[contribute] to building a better world" and to act with "respect for the common interest" by behaving as "responsible members of our communities."

The *Principles* specifically affirm that, far from treating its employees as a simple means of production, the company shows concern for them as individuals. The aim is to "help everyone succeed," to make "our people successful," and to give "our people every opportunity to . . . develop their talents," and "a key responsibilities for managers is to develop their people."

Alongside the focus on sharing, we find another group of values linked to an individual's, or an entity's, self-assertion when facing the outside world. The desire to be the best, which drives the company as a whole, is not presented simply as a way of responding to market pressure but also as being a positive point in itself: "To be the undisputed world leader in building materials," "strengthen this leadership position by being the best," and "achieve worldwide leadership." This desire is a source of ambition. It necessarily implies "involving every employee in this ambition" and "inspiring them [employees] toward a common ambition." This self-assertion does not only involve self-development, but also outperforming others. It means "growing faster than the competition" and being "ahead of our competitors."

Even within the company, each individual is expected to personally assert themselves: "We want all of our employees to be key players in the formulation of their own personal objectives"; "We want all of our people to be able to measure and understand the impact and consequences of their actions."

Reconciling the acclaimed merits of sharing and the desire for self-assertion: the role of cultural references

These two categories of values, which might be described respectively as collectivist and individualistic, are undoubtedly present in all cultures. It would thus appear that they can be qualified as universal. Certainly, it is common practice to oppose individualistic societies and collectivist societies. However, in reality, so-called individualistic societies have a pronounced collectivist dimension and vice versa.[2] This means that each society has to find a way of reconciling the attachment to a high degree of cooperation with individual self-assertion and the desire to come out on top.[3] What differentiates cultures is the way in which individualism and the collectivist spirit are materialized and combined, the areas of life that are more or less affected by either tendency and the type of compromise that creates enough room for both. Lafarge's *Principles* do not simply make a statement of values; they trace a path to reconcile these two tendencies. The reference to values that are independent of time and place thus gives way to a specific, culturally rooted conception of society in which the linkage between the individual and the community (or between a delimited group, particularly companies, and society as a whole) is more or less successfully established.

Although ambition is presented as a value in the *Principles*, this is done in a way that channels and guides it in directions compatible with a certain social order. The aim is to excel, but not at any price; this must be achieved according to the rules, not underhandedly, and by counting on quality and hence on the social utility of what one does.

Emphasis is laid on compliance with the rules: "Our responsibility is ... about complying with local and international laws and standards"; it is good practice to rely "on a limited number of respected and known rules." This compliance goes hand in hand with honest conduct and thus means "respecting the interests of our minority partners." Managers are expected to "evaluate results fairly."

Excelling means producing quality work, which means it is socially useful, rather than acting to the detriment of the community. It is necessary for employees to "innovate," "use their creativity," and contribute "to economic progress." Success is based on "skills," "energy," and the "ability to develop and to demonstrate flexibility, creativity and entrepreneurial spirit." This guarantees the "quality" of what one produces. Everyone has a "commitment to excellence." It is necessary to "continuously improve" and everyone is encouraged to "outperform themselves."

The *Principles* were in fact written at a time when an unswerving faith in the virtues of the market, fuelled by liberal theories, reigned in the business world and beyond. This faith supports the claim that endeavoring to out-distance competitors squares extremely well with pursuing the common good, as "through healthy and vigorous competition" one is "contributing to economic progress."

Conversely, the value attached to community spirit comes in a form compatible with the robust affirmation of the individual, which is also present in the *Principles*.

The concern for employees basically means giving everyone the opportunity to assert themselves individually. It does not involve, for instance, fostering a shared feeling of harmony with the world, or an untroubled professional life. There is, on the other hand, constant mention of the opportunity given to all employees to progress professionally, to assert themselves as autonomous and responsible individuals, to "[develop] talents and potential"; "people act out of conviction"; it is important to give "our people exciting and challenging responsibilities"; "We believe that entrusting people with responsibilities, and not merely tasks, is the best way to leverage their skills, initiatives and motivation."

Moreover, although the *Principles* do indeed say that "[o]utstanding achievements are realized as part of a team effort," the focus is on what each individual contributes through their abilities and actions: it is "through professionalism, personal commitment, shared goals and respect for common rules" on the part of every employee that efficient teamwork "is built daily."

In parallel, although teamwork is celebrated, great importance is attached to employees giving their opinion without fear of conflict. The *Principles* state that divergent views freely expressed—as well as any ensuing conflicts—are not only part and parcel of normal life, but they are also fruitful: "Dealing with conflict is an integral and productive part of teamwork. Teamwork is not about reaching consensus on every issue. It is about each individual contributing, accepting and seeking differences of opinion as a source of progress." And the company expresses its determination to foster an environment in which everyone can "seek to constructively challenge and be challenged." This point is considered important enough to play a major role in the actual organization of the Group: "Managing the tension between 'local' and 'global' is one of the key challenges of our Group and defines the way we are organized."

Lafarge's *Principles* thus combine a reference to values that probably exist worldwide and an indication of how these can be reconciled. This approach, typical of Western societies, is distinctive in the way it connects up individual autonomy and collective unity. People are seen as being legitimately able to assert themselves as individuals by manifesting their desire for personal success, showing their contribution to the common good, defending their opinions and criticizing those of others. They have neither to use oblique means to defend their point of view, nor to expect that a benevolent power will take care of their well-being. Society is made up of a group of individuals who follow their own objectives and defend their own opinions, but these initiatives are channeled so as to remain compatible with a form of common good. The action of each individual is kept in check by an ensemble of rules and regulations enforced by the rule of law. All are bound to act as responsible citizens of a democratic state. Moreover, moral principles are there to encourage people to remain mindful of their fellow citizens. The United States and France offer two different variations of this overall vision of society commonly found in the Western world. The linkage between self-assertion and the need for a form of collective functioning follows a different path in each case: a combination of contractual relations and moral community in the United States and a form of noble allegiance in France. Yet what these two societies have in common made it possible (though not always effortlessly) to produce two versions of the *Principles* that frame similar ways of materializing the values they convey. Both of the paths that the Group takes to present itself make it quite clear that Lafarge is a Western company.

A transfer between cultural worlds

A combination of universal and cultural elements is necessarily part of any approach that a company adopts to promote shared values in its foreign subsidiaries. However, when defining what constitutes sound management practice, it is difficult to know in advance what relates to universal values on the one hand, and to culture-specific perspectives on the other. There is a natural tendency to try to disseminate concurrently the values one upholds and the specific way in which these values take shape in one's own culture. It is only through reactions from employees worldwide that this confusion can be clarified. These make it possible to develop an awareness of what is likely or unlikely to be in resonance with the different mental universes (what is more or less compatible with the prevailing local view in each location of how people should live together) and thus likely to be a source of inspiration in each case. Employee reactions also make it possible to identify what is meaningful to all and thus likely to be truly shared (e.g. a company's concern to apply humane management practices), what is specific to certain parts of the world (e.g. the value placed on discussion), and finally what characterizes a particular context (e.g. an attachment to the autonomy of the skilled professional).

The vagueness of the language used to affirm the corporate values and the fact that words like "sharing," "example," and other relatively abstract words are used with no precise definition in the text offer an effective means of building bridges between what unites and what separates. It is within a cultural setting that a word takes on real meaning and evokes specific realities, concrete behaviors, and tangible forms of life in society. People can always agree over values as long as these are couched in abstract terms, even though the practices they have in mind may be very different. This aspect of language means that it is easy to agree, irrespective of culture, when the discussion is limited to an ideal world. But this gives no indication as to the diversity of what people expect when they come together to organize working jointly.

While extremely different from each other, neither the Chinese nor the Jordanian cultures belong to the family of Western cultures. Individuals in these countries are probably no less attached to their own interests and own opinions than people in Western societies. Yet to have these properly taken into account, they expect a great deal more from a good power that is benevolent and just without shrinking from imposing decisions, that is willing to inform and listen without seeking to enter discussions, and that fully assumes its role of setting an example without the fear of appearing over-directive. Everything in the Group's values that touches on the concern for employees shown by the company and by staff in positions of responsibility has received strong support. However, anything involving the attachment to free expression of opinions and to the clash of ideas has failed to resonate.

At the same time, the image of a benevolent and just power in China is not the same as in Jordan.

In China, the dominant image is one of a bureaucracy managing a system of procedures that stand as the cornerstone of a strict order transcending human intervention. This type of system leads to a rigorous evaluation of each individual's actions. It helps employees to develop, while severely sanctioning their failings. Leaders must be close to their subordinates, to the point of being involved hands-on in the latter's tasks.

In Jordan, the dominant image is rather one of a great leader with a strong profile and high moral authority. It is on him, more than on an administrative body, that people rely to ensure compliance with the rules and fair decisions. Leaders must be close to their troops, informing, consulting, and gracing the workplaces dedicated to menial tasks with their presence, without however feeling obliged to lend a helping hand.

Is this to say that the only way a company can put its values into practice in countries whose cultures differ from the culture prevailing in the place where the parent firm is rooted is to adopt means in harmony with the local culture? What we observed in both China and Jordan shows that the company does in fact have a much wider role to play. In both cases, the local reference is the image of a benevolent and just power, attentive to the well-being of those under its authority. This does not imply, however, that business leaders are consistently true to this image. In both cases, Lafarge took over companies that were far from the mark in this respect. And it is clearly the Group's action that has enabled some sort of virtual ideal to begin to materialize in both the Chinese and Jordanian subsidiaries.

From the corporate world to the world at large

The encounter between shared values and cultural diversity, which we studied in a specific company, is very broadly relevant to today's world: to the corporate world, of course, but also to the world as a whole, caught as it is between a desire for the unity of humankind and the fear of a "clash of civilizations."

National cultures, corporate cultures

In the usual vision of relations between so-called "corporate culture" and the specific cultures of the various countries in which a company operates, one representation predominates. In this representation, a "corporate culture" and a national culture relate to the same order of reality; behaviors common to those who share the same culture are based on common values and common representations. It is thus assumed that when a company sets up in a country the two cultures enter into competition, the question then being which will come out the winner: the local culture with its behaviors, values, and corresponding representations or the corporate culture? And, still according to this widespread representation, the severity of the clash will depend on the magnitude of the "cultural distance" between the local culture and the corporate culture; the greater the difference in behaviors, values, and representations, the harder it will be to establish a linkage.[4]

However, as we have seen throughout this book, the encounter between what is specific to the company and what is specific to the country is of a completely different nature. If we attempt to give the terms "corporate culture" or "national culture" a meaning that fits with what is observed, in neither case are we talking about clearly defined behaviors.

A comparison of Lafarge's actions in China and Jordan clearly shows an emphasis on certain values: concern for people, sharing, and setting an example. And this emphasis is in harmony with the orientations that the Group advocates in its *Principles*. It is therefore justifiable to speak of a common corporate culture. But these values do not materialize in the same way in each country; they do not have the same concrete manifestations and do not translate into the same practices.

Likewise, the unity of a national culture accommodates a wide range of practices associated with very diverse orientations in terms of values. This is especially true when several major systems of competing values, producing very different behaviors, coexist within the same country; this is particularly obvious in Jordan, where religious values exist alongside tribal values, but it can also be seen elsewhere. However, what unites a national culture falls into a different sphere and involves a sort of general framework of meaning. The meaning of events and situations is colored by a particular source of concern: a type of situation that an individual is particularly afraid of encountering and thus tries at all costs to avoid. For instance, in the United States, this involves losing control of your own destiny; in France, being forced to bow down, either through fear or self-interest, to someone with the power to harm you or bestow favors on you; and in China, being caught up in the chaos brought on by an uncontrolled clash of interests and passions (d'Iribarne, 2008). Personal experience is particularly significant whenever it conjures up a person's greatest fear or, on the contrary, wards off the likelihood of it materializing. And the prevailing conception of the right way to behave in society provides a basis for averting the fear in question (in the United States, the ubiquity of contractual relations helps to give individuals the feeling that they do not have to comply with obligations other than those to which they have freely consented and thus that they remain in control of their own destiny).

In this context, the encounter between a "corporate culture" and national cultures is not a competition where the question then becomes which will prevail? If a company wishes to disseminate its culture—understood here as the values it upholds—it should not attempt in its foreign locations to attack the main references that shape the meaning of life in society. It should instead build on these references. And this remains true when a company's action in one of its subsidiaries leads to a work organization that differs vastly from the one most often found in the country concerned.

What we observed in this regard at Lafarge coincides with our findings for other companies. For example, the action taken by STMicroelectronics in its Moroccan subsidiary has led to a sort of moral order that runs counter to what is usually found in companies in the country. This order, however, has taken a specifically Moroccan form in harmony with the conception of a moral order advocated by Moroccan Islam. Similarly, in Danone's Mexican subsidiary, there was a clear influence of the group's values and its "dual project" geared at coupling the company's prosperity with its employees' well-being and with initiatives benefitting the surrounding communities. This was visible in the way the company operated, blending a high degree of mutual support and strong identification with the company, in sharp contrast to what is usually found in Mexican companies. But this organizational practice was specifically Mexican on account of the particular form of relationships that it established both inside the company and between the company and its environment. These relationships successfully averted the main fear marking Mexican culture: that of not being able to achieve one's dreams of grandeur without help, and of not receiving the support that would, despite everything, make these dreams come true (d'Iribarne with Henry, 2007).

Everywhere on the planet, one finds values that seem universal, like mutual care and the importance of close cooperation between people who work together. A company that emphasizes these values, in its words and acts, will be able to put them into practice in its foreign subsidiaries, in a form that is in tune with the local cultural context. This may simply involve opting for certain work methods ordinarily found in the country. However, in societies where it is unusual for cooperative values to hold sway in the corporate world, it may also mean opening up new avenues that call on innovative ways of working together. Western companies that cultivate a humanist tradition are well placed to play this role across much of the world, especially in Asia. Certainly, their values predispose them to exercise a firm, fair, and benevolent authority, which stands as a reference in many societies where these values are rarely put into practice. Such companies can help these societies to engage in a process of economic and social modernization, not only without abandoning their cultures but by adhering more faithfully to the best their cultures have to offer.

The organization of society

For researchers, companies furnish an excellent terrain for observing and analyzing how the encounter between shared values and specific cultures functions. But companies are not the only ones, or even the first, to be concerned by this encounter. It is also present on another scale in the area of national governance, particularly as regards the emergence of democracy and respect for human rights.

Admittedly, the broad questions raised by cultural diversity are well beyond the scope of our topic, be it the question of how society as a whole is organized or the nexus between this diversity and the unity of humankind (we plan to address these issues in another work). Moreover, it could be deemed unfitting to address such "lofty" questions taking a subject as trivial as corporate life as a starting point. But, after all, the great laws of nature are present in the lowliest of phenomena (the laws of gravity apply as much to a falling apple and the flight of a fly as to a cathedral building or planetary movements). Why should it be any different when the subject at hand is humankind? Any ideal that aspires to address humanity will materialize differently depending on how the local culture invests it with meaning. And the phenomena that come into play do not appear to be radically different when it comes to ideals of unequally noble inspiration, be it religion,[5] ideology, state governance, or the management of family or corporate life.

One way out of the untenable dilemma of having to choose between value relativism and cultural imperialism is often called on: a "dialogue of cultures" to help discern what humanity has in common, underlying the diverse visions of what is "good." This would mean reviewing the conceptions of "good" that are supposedly shared by all civilizations— conceptions expressed with different words and different images in different geographies, but which are assumed to have a fundamental oneness all over the world. The "golden rule" is not to do unto others what you would not want others to do unto you or, more positively, do unto others as you would have them do unto you. Is this not common to both Confucius and the Bible, or other forms of ancient wisdom? It would then be up to people of goodwill from the four corners of the earth to unite, over and above all that seems to divide them, and jointly proclaim the values and define the behaviors, institutions, and laws that will bring humanity to live in peace. Yet one question remains un-answered: to what extent is this vision nothing more than pious discourse that can be suitably brought out at innumerable international conferences? More specifically, to what extent and in what form can democracy, human rights, and, more generally, the legacy of the Enlightenment —all of which admittedly involve values but also concrete ways of organizing society—be accepted in societies whose legacies differ from those of Western societies?

These questions begin to emerge whenever a text considered to be as universally applicable as the *Universal Declaration of Human Rights* is translated into various languages. This holds true even in contexts where a text is fully accepted in principle and no attempt is made to promote competing versions such as a "*Universal Islamic Declaration of Human Rights.*" One has only to compare the English and French versions of the *Universal Declaration* to find instances of these questions.

For example, the law and rights are given a greater place in the English version than in the French version:

> Everyone charged with a penal offence *has the right to be* presumed innocent until proved guilty according to law/*Toute personne accusée d'un acte délictueux* est *présumée innocente jusqu'à ce que sa culpabilité ait été légalement établie* (Everyone charged with a penal offence *is* presumed innocent until proved guilty according to law).

Human rights should be protected by *the rule of law/Il est essentiel que les droits de l'homme soient protégés par* un régime de droit (It is essential that human rights be protected by *a legal regime*).

In the first sentence, the English version evokes a procedure based on a legal right that offers its protection to all. However, in the French version, it is no longer a matter of defining a right that one *has*, that one can use to defend oneself, but of what one *is*. In the second sentence, the reference to "a legal regime" supposes recourse to "one" regime, in all its contingency, among many other possible legal regimes. The rule of law is something different. What is invoked in this case is "the" law in all its quintessential majesty.

Similarly, where the French version states that some sort of result will be obtained, the English version is considerably more cautious and speaks rather of efforts to be made:

> The peoples of the United Nations have . . . determined to *promote* . . . better standards of life in larger freedom/*Les peuples des Nations Unies . . . se sont déclarés résolus à . . .* instaurer *de meilleures conditions de vie dans une liberté plus grande* (The peoples of the United Nations have . . . determined to *establish* . . . better living conditions in a larger freedom).
>
> Member States have pledged themselves to *achieve . . . the promotion of* universal *respect* for and observance of human rights . . ./*Les Etats Membres se sont engagés à* assurer . . . le respect *universel et effectif des droits de l'homme . . .* (Member States have pledged themselves to *ensure . . .* the promotion of universal respect for and observance of human rights . . .).

"To promote" is distinctly less categorical than "*instaurer*" (Harrap's translation: "establish") or "*assurer*" (Harrap's translation: "ensure," "guarantee"). This echoes a difference that sets the French and American versions of Lafarge's *Principles* apart. In the Anglo-Saxon approach, there is manifestly a religious and moral perspective marked by human weakness, in which all that matters are good intentions, and a legal perspective involving contractual commitments that must be fulfilled subject to sanction—a terrain to be avoided when there is uncertainty as to the outcome. In a French approach, the reference is rather a sense of honor that excludes any admission of weakness.

These differences between the two versions of the *Universal Declaration* can be seen when one moves from the affirmation of values

("All human beings are born free and equal in dignity and rights") to a description of the means (justice, the state, moral education) used to ensure compliance with these values. The means are embedded in forms of social organization that differ from one country to another. This is the case even for countries as similar as France and the United States in terms of the values they uphold. It is difficult to talk about these values without their basic differences rising to the surface, if only through the nuances in the expressions used to describe them ("promote" or "*instaurer*"). As long as a sufficient level of abstraction is maintained with no precision as to what is understood by the terms used, the vocabulary of values can give the impression that nothing changes when one shifts from one culture to another. However, even the vocabulary used is different when it comes to issues of social organization.

Our incursions into China and the Arab world give an insight into what is likely to materialize with respect to the ideals of human rights. In both cases, we have seen that in these cultures it is difficult to give positive meaning to the confrontation of ideas, whereas this is highly valued in the Enlightenment's powerful message of emancipation. The latter has its roots in European societies or those with a European culture and has taken a particularly radical form in England, France, and the United States.[6] In China or the Arab world, its acceptance and the establishment of pluralistic democracy are problematic issues. In these societies, the presence of a strong and unchallenged power (in China), or a perfect unity between the members of a cohesive group (in Arab countries) is of prime importance given that, in China, the fear of chaos and, in the Arab world, the fear of the humiliation suffered by those in inferior positions are so strong. If one considers that free debate is a *sine qua non* ingredient of a democratic system, there is good reason to be concerned about the future of democracy in these parts of the world. However, if one adopts a diluted vision of democracy whereby what matters is that the ruling power listens to the people and acts with concern for its citizens' welfare, there are grounds for greater optimism.

Thus, in China, the fact that we visited a company and interviewed the employees on its work practices brought us into contact with what ordinary Chinese people—who are neither the henchmen of an authoritarian regime nor the spearheads of pro-democracy struggles—expected with regard to power. Admittedly, their comments did not reveal a conversion to the Western view that power must be challenged. But neither did they adhere to a form of despotism. Although demanding something openly was viewed as aggressive behavior, the hierarchy was expected to read between the lines when subordinates made suggestions. Moreover, the implementation of systems more attentive to employees' opinions was favorably received. Certainly, there was no question of the proud affirmation of citizen power. But it was far from a passive submission to the whims of the powerful, and their core concern within the company was to be in an environment governed by rules. Our observations suggest that when power is exercised on a larger scale, China cannot be expected to normalize its institutions and practices to comply with Western standards, but it can be expected to develop political forms that give greater voice to its people's aspirations. It thus seems possible that Chinese society will evolve towards greater respect for democratic values in a sense that can be qualified broadly or restrictively—depending on whether one wishes to be more or less positive—along lines compatible with its culture.

So why are the values dear to the West more difficult to disseminate in the case of political regimes than in companies? It is because we are not dealing with the same type of exercise of power. When it comes to companies, democracy exists only in a restrictive sense. Moreover, the compatibility between the status of employee and that of a free citizen in a democratic society is seen as problematic in the West. We found traces of this problem in the responses to Lafarge's *Employee Feedback Survey* in France and in the United States. In fact, companies with a humanist tradition still perpetuate a traditional, non-elective corporate power structure, even though their senior management aspires to make the best use of this power. As a result, in the West, these companies are challenged in the name of "true" democracy, being accused at best of paternalism and at worst of hypocrisy. Yet the restrictive form of democracy they propose is remarkably similar to the expectations encountered in much of the world, and not only in China and Jordan. Disseminating a radical version of democracy is another matter. In Western cultures, each individual's right to express their opinion, criticize, and contest is perceived as being an essential rampart against the inhumanity of despotism and slavery. This is by no means the case in all parts of the world. In China, chaos is seen as the main factor leading to inhumanity, and the fear is that any clash of opinions and interests may bring on this chaos. In the Arab world, the sole path ensuring that the highest-placed and lowliest people jointly attain a fully human status seems to be through group unity. In these contexts, the Western model stands little chance of being fully accepted, except by minorities of converts.

Humankind's unity and diversity

What do our observations on the nexus between universal values and cultural specificities suggest about the unity of humankind? An analysis of how the same message transmitting the same values is received and materialized in different cultural settings reveals that this unity is both real and relative.

To take the term "freedom" (*"libertad," "liberté," "Freiheit"*), what is actually understood by this word varies depending on the culture. Anglo-Saxon freedom is closely tied to the idea of ownership; German freedom is seen as having voice in the community; and French freedom is associated with the need to be treated with the respect due to one's rank (d'Iribarne, 2003). And the translation of this term outside the Western world sometimes poses problems.[7] Yet, there clearly seems to be something in common between what an English person, a French person, and a German understand by freedom. For each of them, it has to do with the relationship between the individual and some form of external force (even if this takes the form of negative inclinations that, in another sense, come from inside the person trying to escape them). What is involved is a fight against the influence of this external entity even if, from one culture to another, the entities and the ways of combating their influence are not the same. So when all said and done, it does not seem futile to talk about shared values that transcend cultural diversity. More to the point, when the level of abstraction is set high enough, we have to hand a vocabulary of values enabling us to build bridges between languages and thus between cultures, and identify values that have meaning everywhere. However, this unity of values needs to be understood in a much looser sense than that which comes to mind when we imagine humanity governed by common rules, a common law, and similar institutions.

Finally, what can be said about the much debated issue of the clash of civilizations? Can we go beyond ready-made opinions and bellicose or pacific slogans and devote rigorous thought to the role that cultural diversity plays in the world's destiny? This will require a great deal of effort, far beyond that seen in the corporate world. However, our observations in China and Jordan do open up some avenues for exploration. We encountered some productive forms of cooperation that, to succeed, did not entail eliminating cultural differences between the partners, Westerners on one side, Chinese and Jordanians on the other. It thus seems hard to believe that a culture gap inevitably gives rise to conflict. At the same time, this encounter took place on particularly favorable ground (cooperation between a Western company with a humanist tradition and employees in search of a "good power"). Other spheres (such as the UN Commission for Human Rights, then the UN Human Rights Council) are much less fertile. The error would doubtless be to consider that conflict, or cooperation, is inherent to the encounter between two cultures, whatever the circumstances. Or again to believe that the only factors at play are those that touch on competing or complementary interests, and that values or cultures have no role to play. These views are obviously far too simplistic. But, much remains to be done if we are to reach a clear understanding of how cultural differences intervene in the different areas where cultures come to meet.

Notes

1   For a more in-depth analysis of how modern societies, despite their pluralist values and practices and their evolution over time, nonetheless have a culture that is both shared by their members and lasting cf. d'Iribarne, 2008.

2   For example, H. Triandis (1995: 2), an authority in the field, states:

> In recent years, social psychologists have made numerous attempts to measure tendencies toward individualism and collectivism, and in doing so they discovered considerable complexity in what should be included in these constructs. They have also theorised about the causes and consequences of people's behaving in individualistic and collectivist ways and discovered that people are typically both individualists and collectivists.

3   In the corporate sector, special focus has been placed on the complexity of this reconciliation using comparisons between organizational models typical of the United States, where there is a strong concern to highlight the individual's contribution to collective work, and those in which the collective side of performance is more emphasized, as in Japan. The difficulties that the American automotive industry experienced in implementing lessons from Japan in the area of production methods—lessons that are nonetheless widely recognized as commendable by the industry—are a good example of the tension that exists between the recognition of an individual's uniqueness and the strength of the community (Womack *et al.*, 1990).

4   The questions posed by the linkage between more or less universal values and cultural specificity can also be seen when religions develop in different cultural contexts. One example is the famous Chinese Rites Controversy that marked Catholicism's attempt at inculturation in seventeenth-century China. Here again, when it comes to collaborative work, there seem to be many commonalities with the issues raised by this linkage.

5   This view is well expressed by Kostova and Roth (2002).

6   Concerning the fact that this message took on a more radical form there than in Germany (Gadamer, 1992 [1960]).

7   This is the case for the Chinese translation of "freedom" (Vandermeersch, 2004: 185).

Conclusion

There is a whole conception of culture, deeply rooted in people's minds and associated with values, behaviors, and identity, which gives rise to a very negative view of cultural differences and the role these play in the relations between peoples. These differences are seen as fraught with confrontations in a war of values. In particular, the nexus between democracy and human rights on the one hand and cultural diversity on the other hand raises many questions. It seems intolerable to think that these values could lastingly remain the prerogative of some. It is equally intolerable to imagine that the West's mission is to accelerate "progress" in cultures that view such values with an unfavorable eye. Companies that develop their business across the world are faced with the same questions. A cultural imperialism that is morally dubious in its inspiration and of questionable efficiency with respect to consequences does not appear to be any more acceptable than a "respect for cultures" that is akin to abdication.

To escape from the malaise spawned by these difficulties, it is tempting to altogether abolish the idea that a people can indeed have its own specific culture and to imagine humanity as a melting pot in which each individual pieces together a sort of personal culture *à la carte* from scraps of cultures that once had some consistency but which have now become totally fluid, thus eliminating all risk of confrontation between cultural blocks. Between fearfulness and utopian dreams, there remains little room for a meaningful analysis of what cultures really are and what role they play. And it is thus highly likely that the question of the linkage between the assumed universality of values and cultural diversity will be addressed only in terms of wishful thinking.

To break out of wishful thinking, we need to leave the celestial realm of ideas and come back down to earth: take an interest in what actually happens when people whose world vision has been shaped by different cultures come together to work collectively; choose a field of observation;

watch, analyze, try to understand. To begin with, what happens when values are expressed in different languages? What remains thereafter that is truly shared and what form of differentiation begins to emerge? And what happens when we take one step further into the real world and create forms of organization in order for values to have a real impact on life? In what way do the diverse conceptions of living together harmoniously then influence the ways we go about it?

We have endeavored to answer these questions by looking at four cultural universes: on the one hand, the United States and France, which have played a significant role in the advent of democracy and human rights; on the other hand, China and Jordan (taken as an example of a Middle-Eastern country), both countries where these values are not particularly applied. We studied the approach used by a global firm with French roots and a strong American component to foster shared values in the two non-Western countries. And we sought to learn from our observations.

When Chinese or Jordanians work in the subsidiary of a foreign company, they do not forget their own culture: a specific view of life leading to a distinctive conception of what living together harmoniously means, and notably a singular vision of how power should be exercised. This conception is the yardstick by which they judge what they experience and, more specifically, what they receive from the outside world. But contrary to what a common view of cultural differences would suggest, this in no way prevents them from appreciating what comes from elsewhere.

In China and Jordan alike, a great deal is expected of a "good power," which is seen as being close, just, and concerned for those under its responsibility. Yet, based on what our interviewees told us, day-to-day life in local companies bears little resemblance to the local image of a good power (in China, a bureaucracy guaranteeing a strict order; in Jordan, a great leader with strong moral authority who ensures that fairness is respected). They are more accustomed to a distant, arbitrary, and indifferent power. This is because, although culture shapes the image of a good power, it leaves the wide open question of what leaders actually do with this image. Whether or not the image is faithfully upheld depends on values and not culture.

It just so happens that Western companies with a humanist tradition include among their values the responsibility of power. They consider that, ideally, this power must be close, just, and concerned for the well-being of those under its authority. Certainly, their vision of this power is also marked by culture. Culture determines the different ways in which the image of this power materializes in each country. However, if this type of humanist-oriented company wishes to remain true to its own values wherever it sets up, and if it is also willing to put these into practice, at the same time integrating the local view of a good power, it is likely to garner strong support from its employees in all societies where much is expected from a good power. It can even expect this support to be stronger in these countries than in Western countries, where the image of a good power is viewed with a degree of suspicion and is in danger of being accused of paternalism, even hypocrisy. In a large part of the world, this possibility opens up vast prospects for improving the efficiency of companies and the economic development of countries.

The situation is different when we look at another category of values: those that are unrelated to the ideal of a good power in general, but involve more specifically the ideal of a fully democratic society characterized by the attachment to freedom of thought, criticism of others' viewpoints, and lively debate. While these values are highly prized in the West, this is far from the case in a good part of the world. And this is not simply because they are rejected by leaders who are greedy for dictatorship. A deeper reason, which showed up very clearly in our investigations, is that for the majority of people they are seen not so much as values as a cause for fear. They are seen as bringing division and chaos rather than a greater humaneness. If a company with Western roots aims to promote these values worldwide, the likelihood is that it be neither understood nor accepted in a good many places.

This distinction between the values relating, on one side, to the image of a good power and, on the other, to the image of a democratic society is a crucial one when one moves from the corporate world to a country scale. It is one thing to try and spread what could be described as a restrictive version of democracy, implying equality before the law, the leaders' relative capacity to listen to their people, and a use of power that is reasonably congruent with the public good. As long as this is what is being defended, it is possible to build on values doubtless encountered all over the world, even though these are often betrayed by reality. However, it is another thing to set out to diffuse a radical version of democracy centered on individual rights, freedom of thought, and the importance of critical debate. In this area, the West will continue to pursue a largely solitary path unless much of the world undergoes deep cultural changes and, on a not-too-distant horizon, it would be very optimistic to count on these.

Appendix: national cultures and management

An interpretative approach

The research presented in this book is one phase in a broader program that aims to progressively build up an inventory of what, within national cultures, concerns the functioning of organizations. Based on an interpretative approach (d'Iribarne, 2011), this has led to us to carry out numerous case studies, so far covering about fifty countries across every continent. The initial research compared three plants owned, or until recently owned, by the same industrial group and respectively located in the United States, the Netherlands, and France (d'Iribarne, 1989). Subsequently, investigations were conducted into two types of cases: situations where management tools are used in a cultural context other than the one in which they were originally conceived, and situations involving the functioning of multicultural organizations (d'Iribarne *et al.*, 1998; d'Iribarne with Henry, 2007; Segal, 2009). We have also examined the role culture plays when translating a text into different languages (Chapter 1 of this book). During our research, we met with the various challenges, both theoretical and methodological, that arise when one attempts to delimit or define what a common culture can be within modern society. After a good deal of searching, it has finally seemed possible to overcome these difficulties (d'Iribarne, 2008).

An interpretative approach to national cultures

The idea of shared meaning is at the heart of interpretative approaches to culture. However, this formulation makes it difficult to imagine even the possibility of there being shared cultures within modern societies. This is because, first, meaning is not just received but also produced and, second, society is divided into distinct social groups. The salient role of actors in sense-making has been highlighted by a major field of study (Garfinkel, 1967). Hence Staber (2006: 192) expresses the widely held point of view that "[c]ulture-based understandings are not a static, pre-existing condition that can be seen as exerting a simple causal influence on action. They are themselves fundamentally constructed phenomena that arise and are sustained or adjusted through social interaction." But, if everything is constantly being renegotiated, this can only be done at a local level and it is hard to see what can be sustained on a large scale. Besides, within a society, rival definitions of reality coexist even if there are also dominant definitions (Berger and Luckmann, 1966). From this perspective, the idea of a national culture has to be rejected, and can even be accused of hiding domination behind a mask of unity (Alvesson, 2002).

In our own research, we have not come across shared ways of reacting and responding to situations in the societies where we conducted our investigations. As a result, we have not been able to use conceptions of culture borrowed from the available literature on the subject, since these are too closely tied to the idea of community (*Gemeinschaft*) to be applicable to heterogeneous groups. What finally emerged was that a shared framework of meaning can indeed be found within the same society (d'Iribarne, 2008). What is striking is that a certain vision of what constitutes the proper way of living together does indeed exist. This vision is linked to a certain conception of authority, freedom, dignity, duty, and negotiating conflicting points of view. It defines the border-line between what is considered acceptable and unacceptable in terms of constraint (obligation), risk, and criticism. It is by referring to this vision that actors can give meaning to what they experience. Each society's ideal vision of harmonious coexistence is incessantly present in the background when people talk about their experiences, whether these are positive or negative. This vision does not however directly determine social practices, and significant deviations from the ideal are to be found. Yet considerable efforts are made to arrange daily reality, with varying degrees of success, using this vision as a reference point. This is not to say that actors are conscious of this vision or that they are able to explain it in clear terms. It remains in some way implicitly self-evident. It is up to the researcher to make out its contours.

At this stage of analysis, it is already possible to gain deeper insight into what differentiates organizational forms in various societies. But this alone does not afford an understanding of the extent to which the actors are attached to a certain way of living together. To understand this side of things, we need to delve much further (d'Iribarne, 2008, 2009).

Differences in how societies organize the way people work together, and more broadly live together, may be understood in terms of two dimensions. On the one hand, a basic apprehension (understood as a cause for concern sparking unease or even anxiety) that is shared by all the members of a society and plays a key role in the collective imagination that invests social life with meaning; this apprehension, in turn, drives the search for a means of deliverance enabling them to avoid it. On the other hand, representations that associate everyday situations with either the cause for concern or with the experience of being protected from it.

Dovetailing these two dimensions, we can then understand how, within a given society, change is coupled to stability and diversity to commonality. The opposition between a fundamental cause for concern and the corresponding means of deliverance provides a framework of meaning that is both common and remarkably stable when examined historically. Yet, the meaning given to a situation that evokes a cause for concern or, on the contrary, a way of averting it is subject to conflicting debate and evolves over time. It is the subject both of ideological struggles between actors seeking to influence the meaning given to events and situations and of debates that impact how society is organized.

Organizational life spawns situations to which it is difficult to attribute positive meaning, since they are associated with an apprehension or fear. Combining representations and practices helps to throw a positive light onto these otherwise problem-ridden situations by assimilating them to a positive experience (i.e. the experience of being protected from the fundamental cause for concern). To a large extent, this means disguising realities likely to generate a degree of anxiety. At the same time, practices need to be organized in such a way that these realities mirror the images one wants to associate with them as authentically as possible, ensuring they have a maximum of features in common with these images.

For instance, American society has lastingly ascribed great significance to finding oneself at the mercy of someone else; this fear can be appeased as long as an individual feels that they are in full command of their own destiny, much like an owner who controls their estate or property. In the United States, organizations tend to be highly structured, both in terms of language and practices, so as to avert the dreaded image of being dependent on someone else's will. The importance placed on contractual relations allows society to reach this goal. In French society, the fundamental apprehension is being forced to kowtow, through fear or interest, to someone with the power either to harm you or shower you with favors. This fear can be avoided as long as an individual is treated with the consideration due to their rank, or if they fight to defend their dignity. Again, in France, reference to a *métier*,[1] to an *homme de métier* (a professional), and the inherent nobility of a *métier* with all its related representations and practices, including the concomitant rights and duties, helps to assuage the fear of finding oneself in a position deemed servile. Relationships with authority and customers tend to be organized and spoken of in a way that allows them to be associated mostly with positive images.

In different parts of the world, one finds other areas of anxiety that are sometimes surprising to an outside observer. In Cameroon, the fear of hostile maneuverings obscurely hatched by people who put on a pleasant face with you has a strong impact on social relations (d'Iribarne with Henry, 2007). In Bali, the fear of being submerged by the chaos that could be unleashed by the collective loss of emotional self-control occupies a pivotal place (Geertz, 1973).

A form of investigation

What a person says when asked about any kind of activity involving interactions with others, particularly concerning their worklife, does not only inform us about the actual functioning of the activity in question (for example, a given procedure relying on a particular IT system used to manage a specific relationship between two departments). It also gives us access to the two levels of culture that interest us. By comparing the remarks made by different actors on various areas of life, we are able to capture what characterizes a culture.

First of all, their remarks afford relatively direct access to the ideal forms of living together that people sharing the same culture use to give meaning to and judge their life experiences; one can identify, in varying degrees of completeness and detail, portraits of a good or bad superior, of someone that can be trusted or not, a fair or unfair way of judging, a satisfying or unsatisfying decision process, etc. Elements of this portrait are present, at least implicitly, the moment that a judgment is made about a situation, action or individual, or when someone tries to present a situation, action, or individual in a favorable or unfavorable light.

Moreover, what people say when describing either themselves or situations they find themselves in teems with traces, often far from obvious, of the obsessions (fears and ways of averting these fears) that characterize the society whose culture they share.

These traces can be collected simply by conducting a series of interviews with people working in an organization. From a method-ological point of view, interview questions should not make direct reference to culture, as the underlying beliefs structuring each and every one of the interviewee's responses is generally the last thing they are able to explain. Besides, if people are asked to speak freely in their own terms about their work, preoccupations, challenges or how they overcome these, then clues to the culture they are immersed in are bound to surface. Their conversations are full of clues to the implicit vision that they use to judge what surrounds them. Similarly, one can find expressions that reveal the apprehensions inhabiting the person speaking and the ways used to assuage these. Traces of these elements can also be found in written documents produced within the organizations themselves (annual reports, corporate guidelines, and communication documents).

These elements become perceptible as soon as an interviewee is asked to speak generally about their work. The discussion can be narrowed down through more specific questions focused, for example, on delegation and control processes, the roll-out of an IT system, quality procedures, a code of ethics, customer relations policy, etc. At this stage of the investigation, the most important thing is to remain open to each individual's preoccupations and to the way in which these are expressed.

Generally speaking, once one has detected how to decipher what is unique to a specific culture, it is easy to identify this particularity in any interview or written material. However, a salient question to be addressed is how to bring these cultural references to light when one does not yet know what they could actually be. Here we are dealing with a classic hermeneutic circle (Gadamer, 1992 [1960]). The clues that have been assembled can only take on their full meaning when they fall into place in the overall picture, and this big picture is in turn built up from these clues. The results are only convincing when several features, seemingly ill-matched or disparate at first glance, begin to take shape in a way that is felt to be coherent and make sense. Before arriving at this coherence, one may have to blindly feel one's way forward laboriously and lengthily. The general method here would be to gather the first clues of what one wishes to bring to light and use them to build up a tentative global picture. Subsequently one continues to look for clues, this time with the insight provided by the initial global picture, going back and forth between these two closely interconnected, yet analytically distinct steps.

An essential step, which unfortunately does not correspond to any foolproof method, consists in forming conjectures that lead to an overall hypothetical interpretation of all the clues assembled. This abductive process (Peirce, 1934–48) is similar to that of trying to solve a criminal investigation from a series of clues. The quality of the results will largely depend on the pertinence of the conjecture. The second step involves verifying whether all of the clues are a good fit with the initial hypothesis. If they are not, new conjectures will need to be formed.

What allows us to move from a small number of interviews to a culture considered in its entirety is the extreme coherence of the data; normally in a case study, the ideal ways of living and working together, as well as the cause for concern that plays a pivotal role in the society under study, are observable in each and every interview. When this is not the case, we are clearly dealing with multicultural societies containing very distinct populations.

In an ethnographic study, the question arises as to how the specificities truly shared on a national scale can be distinguished from those that, by contrast, are specific to only a small locality (a company or a plant). From experience, we can advance three responses to this question.

First, the diversity of the people one is likely to meet within a small-sized entity such as an industrial organization should not be underestimated, and what they have in common does not only reflect something specific to that group. For instance, we carried out a study in an aluminum plant located in a small town in Maryland (d'Iribarne, 1989). There we met a wide diversity of people. Some had worked in a sister plant on the west coast. Many had rather complicated professional and geographic backgrounds. We spoke to engineers, workers, managers, trades unionists, whites, blacks, young, and not so young people. Most were men, though there were a few women. What they had in common could not therefore have stemmed from the singularities of a particular group. It appeared that what they shared could be found across the whole of American society; it was because they all belonged to this society that they had something in common despite all of their differences.

It is true (and this is the second point) that one sometimes encounters a company with a very distinct culture, which introduces another trait common to the interviewees, in addition to the fact that they all live in the same country. This was the case, for instance, in the investigations we conducted in Mexico and Morocco (d'Iribarne, 2003). However, it was not difficult to distinguish the particularities of the companies studied from the characteristics of the country in general. In both cases, the majority of those we met had not pursued their careers in the same company. In addition, some individuals (sometimes the same ones) had known the company at a time when it was run very differently. When talking to us, they constantly highlighted the exceptional aspects of their company.

Finally (the third point), the fact that we could match up our field observations with data from other research areas, provides us with an extra safeguard. Similarly, we can examine whether the conceptions of life in society that we identified fit with that society's political institutions. If today we find in an American factory conceptions analogous to those penned in *The Federalist* (Hamilton *et al.*, 1992 [1787–8]) or in Locke (1960 [1690]), it would be difficult to consider this simply as a chance happening.

Note

1 One's professional role or field of expertise. In France people commonly perceive their work in a similar way to that of American professionals, such as lawyers and doctors (translator's note).

References

Alvesson, M. (2002) *Understanding organizational culture*, London: Sage.

Balazs, E. (1988 [1968]) *La bureaucratie céleste. Recherches sur l'économie et la société de la Chine traditionnelle*, Paris: Gallimard, coll. "Tel."

Berger, P. and Luckmann, T. (1966) *The social construction of reality*, New York: Doubleday.

Charillon, F. and Kassay, A. (2002) "Jordanie: le Charisme monarchique à réinventer," in R. Leveau and A. Hammoudi (eds) *Monarchies arabes: Transitions et dérives dynastiques*, Notes et études documentaires, no. 5158–9, September, la Documentation française.

Collomb, B. (2007) "Entreprise internationale et diversités culturelles," *La Jaune et la Rouge*, April, pp. 8–11.

Confucius (1971 [1893]) *The analects*, trans. J. Legge, Mineola, NY: Dover Publications.

Duan, M. (2007) "Incomplétude des contrats et relations inter-firmes dans une économie en transition: le cas de la Chine," doctoral dissertation, Université Paris X Nanterre.

Gadamer, H.-G. (1992 [1960]) *Truth and method*, 2nd rev. edn., trans. J. Weinsheimer and D. G. Marshall, New York: Crossroad.

Garfinkel, H. (1967) *Studies in ethnomethodology*, Englewood Cliffs, NJ: Prentice-Hall.

Geertz, C. (1968) *Islam observed: Religious development in Morocco and Indonesia*, Chicago, IL: University of Chicago Press.

Geertz, C. (1973) "Person, time and conduct in Bali," *The interpretation of culture*, New York: Basic Books.

Granet, M. (1994 [1929]) *La civilisation chinoise*, Paris: Albin Michel.

Hamilton, A., Madison, J., and Jay, J. (1992 [1787–8]) *The Federalist, or the New Constitution*, London: Everyman.

Harzing, A.-W. (2002) "The interaction between language and culture: A test of the cultural accommodation hypothesis in seven countries," *Language and Intercultural Communication*, vol. 2, no. 2, pp. 120–39.

Hofstede, G. (1981) *Culture's consequences*, 1st edn., London: Sage.

Hofstede, G. (2001) *Culture's consequences*, 2nd edn., London: Sage.

Ibn Khaldûn (1967 [1377–1402]) *The Muqqdimah: An introduction to history*, ed. and trans. F. Rosenthal, Princeton, NJ: Princeton University Press.

d'Iribarne, P. (1989) *La logique de l'honneur*, Paris: Seuil.

d'Iribarne, P. (2002) "La légitimité de l'entreprise comme acteur éthique aux Etats-Unis et en France," *Revue française de gestion*, vol. 28, no. 140, September–October, pp. 23–39.

d'Iribarne, P. (2003) "Trois figures de la liberté," *Annales*, vol. 58, no. 5, pp. 953–78.

d'Iribarne, P. (2006) *L'étrangeté française*, Paris: Seuil.

d'Iribarne, P. (2008) *Penser la diversité du monde*, Paris: Seuil.

d'Iribarne, P. (2009) "National cultures and organizations in search of a theory: An interpretative approach," *International Journal of Cross-Cultural Management*, vol. 9, no. 3, pp. 309–21.

d'Iribarne, P. (2011) "How to use ethnographical case studies to decipher national cultures," in R. Piekkari and C. Welch (eds.), *Rethinking the case study in international business and management research*, Cheltenham, UK: Edward Elgar.

d'Iribarne, P. with Henry, A. (2007) *Successful companies in the developing world: Managing in synergy with cultures*, Notes et Documents no. 36, Paris: Agence Française de Développement. Accessed from www.afd.fr/home/publications/travaux-de-recherche/archives-anciennescollections/Notes Documents on March 27, 2012.

d'Iribarne, P., Henry, A., Segal, J.-P., Chevrier, S., and Globokar, T. (1998) *Cultures et mondialisation*, Paris: Seuil.

Jullien, F. with Marchaisse, T. (2000) *Penser d'un dehors (la Chine): Entretiens d'extrême-occident*, Paris: Seuil.

Kostova, T. and Roth, K. (2002) "Adoption of an organizational practice by subsidiaries of multinational corporations: Institutional and relational effects," *Academy of Management Journal*, vol. 45, no. 1, pp. 215–33.

Locke, J. (1960 [1690]) *Two treatises of government*, ed. Peter Laslett, Cambridge, UK: Cambridge University Press.

Montesquieu, Baron de, Charles Louis de Secondat (1777) *The complete works of M. de Montesquieu*, London: T. Evans, 4 vols. Accessed from http://oll.libertyfund.org on October 2, 2011.

Peirce, C. S. (1934–48) *Collected papers*, 4 vols., Cambridge, MA: Harvard University Press.

Peters, T. J. and Waterman Jr., R. (1982) *In search of excellence*, New York: Harper and Row.

Pickthall, M. W. (trans. and ed.) (1992) *The meaning of the glorious Qur'an*, New York: Everyman's Library, Random House USA Inc.

Segal, J.-P. (2009) *Efficaces, ensemble*, Paris: Seuil.

Staber, U. (2006) "Social capital processes in cross cultural management," *International Journal of Cross Cultural Management*, vol. 6, pp. 189–203.

Tréguer-Felten, G. (2009) "Le leurre de l'anglais lingua franca? Une étude comparative de documents professionnels produits en anglais par des locuteurs chinois, français et américains," doctoral disseration, Paris 3-Sorbonne nouvelle.

Triandis, H. C. (1995) *Individualism and collectivism*, Boulder, CO: Westview Press.

Troeltsch, E. (1958 [1912]) *Protestantism and progress*, Boston, MA: Beacon Press.

Usinor Group (1998) *Aciers*, no. 38, March, Usinor Group.

Vandermeersch, L. (2004) *Le nouveau monde sinisé*, Paris: Librairie Young-Feng.

Vernant, J.-P. (1962) *Les origines de la pensée grecque*, Paris: PUF.

Weber, M. (2002 [1920]) "Protestant sects and the spirit of capitalism," in *The protestant ethic and the spirit of capitalism*, Hoboken, NJ: Wiley-Blackwell.

Womack, J. P., Jones, D. T., and Roos, D. (1990) *The machine that changed the world*, New York, Toronto: Rawson Associates, Collier Macmillan Canada, and Maxwell Macmillan International.

Yousfi, H. (2007) "Gérer en Jordanie: une coexistence problématique entre système hiérarchique et idéal réligieux d'une communauté d'égaux," *Revue Française de Gestion*, no. 171, February, pp. 157–73.

Zghal, R. (1994) *La culture de la dignité et le flou de l'organisation; culture et comportement organisationnel*, Tunis: Centre d'études, de recherche et de publications.

Index

Taylor & Francis

eBooks

FOR LIBRARIES

ORDER YOUR
FREE 30 DAY
INSTITUTIONAL
TRIAL TODAY!

Over 23,000 eBook titles in the Humanities,
Social Sciences, STM and Law from some of the
world's leading imprints.

Choose from a range of subject packages or create your own!

Benefits for **you**

▶ Free MARC records
▶ COUNTER-compliant usage statistics
▶ Flexible purchase and pricing options

Benefits for your **user**

▶ Off-site, anytime access via Athens or referring URL
▶ Print or copy pages or chapters
▶ Full content search
▶ Bookmark, highlight and annotate text
▶ Access to thousands of pages of quality research
  at the click of a button

For more information, pricing enquiries or to order
a free trial, contact your local online sales team.

UK and Rest of World: **online.sales@tandf.co.uk**

US, Canada and Latin America:
e-reference@taylorandfrancis.com

www.ebooksubscriptions.com

Taylor & Francis **eBooks**
Taylor & Francis Group

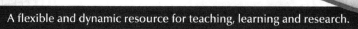
A flexible and dynamic resource for teaching, learning and research.